SPORTS ENCYCLOPEDIAS

THE PROFESSIONAL WRESTLING ENCYCLOPEDIA

BY MARY GERARD

Encyclopedias

An Imprint of Abdo Reference

abdobooks.com

TABLE OF CONTENTS

HISTORY

Early wrestlers often showcased their skills at exhibitions or circuses. In the 1840s, French showman Jean Exbrayat organized one of the first wrestling troupes.

ORIGINS OF PRO WRESTLING

People have been taking part in wrestling competitions for thousands of years. The form of entertainment now known as professional wrestling began in Europe in the 1800s. In the 1830s, some wrestlers in France formed troupes. They traveled around the country to compete in front of audiences. The wrestlers were presented by showmen, who gave them nicknames when introducing them. The showmen offered prizes to audience members who could knock the wrestlers down.

Soon, organizers began predetermining which wrestlers would win matches based on who the audience wanted to win. This allowed the most popular wrestler to win. This practice was called "fixing" and was later referred to as "kayfabe." Audiences knew the winner was preselected, but this didn't hurt wrestling's popularity. Professional wrestling spread throughout Europe. It was known as Greco-Roman wrestling due to its Greek and Roman origins.

In the mid-1800s, pro wrestling made its way to the United States, where people were looking for new forms of entertainment. Early participants included college students who hoped to make money by wrestling in carnivals. Wrestling soon became as well-liked as boxing and baseball.

However, its popularity didn't last. Many fans suspected that wrestling matches were not real fights. As more of these wrestling events became staged performances, many Americans lost interest in the sport.

French wrestler Paul Pons, nicknamed "The Colossus," became famous during the 1890s. He won a World Greco-Roman Wrestling Championship in 1898.

THE GOLD DUST TRIO

Wrestling had a resurgence of popularity during the 1920s. The Gold Dust Trio was one reason why. This group was made up of three wrestling promoters, Ed "Strangler" Lewis, Billy Sandow, and Joseph Raymond "Toots" Mondt. They began organizing wrestling matches in the United States. The matches featured numerous wrestlers.

Lewis was a world champion competitive wrestler. He partnered with wrestler Mondt and manager Sandow to introduce new concepts to pro wrestling. The trio created storylines for wrestlers that unfolded throughout numerous matches, which attracted new viewers and kept them engaged

Ed "Strangler" Lewis, *left*, was one of the most successful wrestlers of the 1920s and 1930s. He was known for his wrestling rivalry with Joe Stecher, *right*.

Boxer Jack Dempsey, *left*, and wrestler Joe Stecher, *right*, were popular sports stars during the 1920s and 1930s.

with the show. The trio scripted conflicts between wrestlers and kept the same competitors around over longer periods of time to develop their storylines. This allowed fans to get familiar with wrestlers as the show traveled to various cities. It offered a way for wrestlers to grow their fan base too.

The Gold Dust Trio showcased new wrestling moves and tag team matches, or matches with multiple wrestlers. The trio also scripted roles for wrestling referees to give them a bigger presence in matches. The referees added to storylines and interacted with the audience. These changes attracted new fans and created more excitement around the sport.

Lou Thesz, *left*, competed in many NWA matches during the mid-1900s. He won the NWA World Heavyweight Championship three times.

THE TERRITORIES ERA

From 1948 to 1980, several pro-wrestling organizations formed in the United States. The three main promotions were the National Wrestling Alliance (NWA), the American Wrestling Association (AWA), and the World Wide Wrestling Federation (WWWF). During this period, pro wrestling was organized into regional groups known as territories. Different organizations were popular in different regions of the United States.

All three organizations were extremely popular in the 1950s, and they gained TV contracts to further promote the sport. People all over the country could watch wrestling events on TV, which attracted new fans. However, wrestling began receiving so much TV coverage that fans started to get bored with it in the 1960s. The NWA, AWA, and WWWF competed against one another and advertised during the others' events. Soon, wrestling was mostly shown in filler spots on late-night TV.

By the 1970s, fewer fans attended events, and wrestling promoters struggled to make money. Some were even going out of business. Despite pro wrestling's struggles during this time, the era produced several famous wrestlers. Some of the most popular were Verne Gagne, Bruno Sammartino, and André the Giant.

André the Giant, *right*, became a popular pro-wrestling star in the 1970s. In 1976, he joined boxer Chuck Wepner, *left*, for a boxer vs. wrestler match.

RISE OF THE WWF

In 1979, the WWWF rebranded to become the World Wrestling Federation (WWF). Three years later, Vince McMahon bought the WWF from his father, Vincent J. McMahon. The younger McMahon soon made changes to how he promoted the WWF and boosted pro wrestling back into the mainstream.

In 1983, the WWF gained a network television contract. This increased WWF's exposure and made it the most popular pro-wrestling organization. McMahon broadcast WWF matches, recruited wrestlers from other organizations, and sold wrestling merchandise throughout the United States. This turned wrestling into a national form of entertainment.

McMahon also created popular wrestling characters, such as Hulk Hogan. Hogan's fan base quickly grew, and his fans became known as Hulkamaniacs. Hogan and pro wrestling became wildly popular.

McMahon took advantage of this popularity and created pay-per-view (PPV) events. Audiences could pay an extra fee to watch shows at home on television. WrestleMania was the most popular PPV event. It was first held on March 31, 1985. In the main event, Hogan teamed up with actor Mr. T and

Vince McMahon originally worked as a wrestling announcer for WWF. He was 37 years old when he bought the company from his father.

The first WrestleMania event took place at Madison Square Garden in New York City. During the main event, Mr. T hoisted opponent "Rowdy" Roddy Piper up on his shoulders.

"Superfly" Jimmy Snuka. They defeated "Rowdy" Roddy Piper, "Mr. Wonderful" Paul Orndorff, and "Cowboy" Bob Orton.

PPV events were a huge success. WrestleMania III in 1987 became one of the most-watched wrestling events in history. During the event, Hogan defeated André the Giant, ending André's 15-year winning streak. A record number of 93,173 fans attended the event.

WCW star Goldberg, *top*, pins opponent Scott Hall during a 1998 match.

THE RAGING 1990s

In the mid-1990s, WWF's popularity began to fade. This opened the door for new pro-wrestling organizations to compete for audiences. In 1988, media mogul Ted Turner created World Championship Wrestling (WCW). It quickly became popular. WCW attracted fans by bringing in stars such as Ric Flair. It also developed new stars such as Goldberg and Sting. But the biggest shock came in 1994. That year, Hulk Hogan left WWF and joined WCW. These stars helped WCW develop an enormous fan base. It eventually surpassed WWF. WCW was on top of the TV ratings from May 1996 until March 1998.

Meanwhile, Extreme Championship Wrestling (ECW) promoted itself as the most daring wrestling league.

Entertainers used weapons during matches, including barbed wire, chairs, and tables. These dangerous antics appealed to fans. Though never as popular as WWF, the ECW developed a loyal following. The organization also produced popular wrestlers such as Raven, the Sandman, Cactus Jack, and Sabu.

THE nWo

In 1996, former WWF wrestlers Scott Hall and Kevin Nash "invaded" WCW. Soon Hulk Hogan joined them. Eventually their New World Order (nWo) grew into a popular stable. A stable is a group of wrestlers who form a partnership. The nWo played a big role in WCW overtaking WWF in TV ratings.

Many wrestlers who competed in ECW, such as "Cactus Jack" Mick Foley, went on to compete for other wrestling organizations.

WWE DOMINANCE

The rise of WCW threatened WWF. To win back audiences, the WWF developed an edgier show. This approach helped WWF return to the top. Before long, it was the only major pro-wrestling organization left. In 2001, WWF acquired the struggling WCW organization. ECW also struggled financially. It declared bankruptcy in 2001, and WWF purchased it.

In 2002, WWF's name changed to World Wrestling Entertainment (WWE). This name change avoided confusion between the wrestling organization and the World Wildlife Fund. The Fund also went by the acronym WWF.

RISE OF WOMEN'S WRESTLING

During this time, women's wrestling started gaining popularity. For years, women had played only minor wrestling roles,

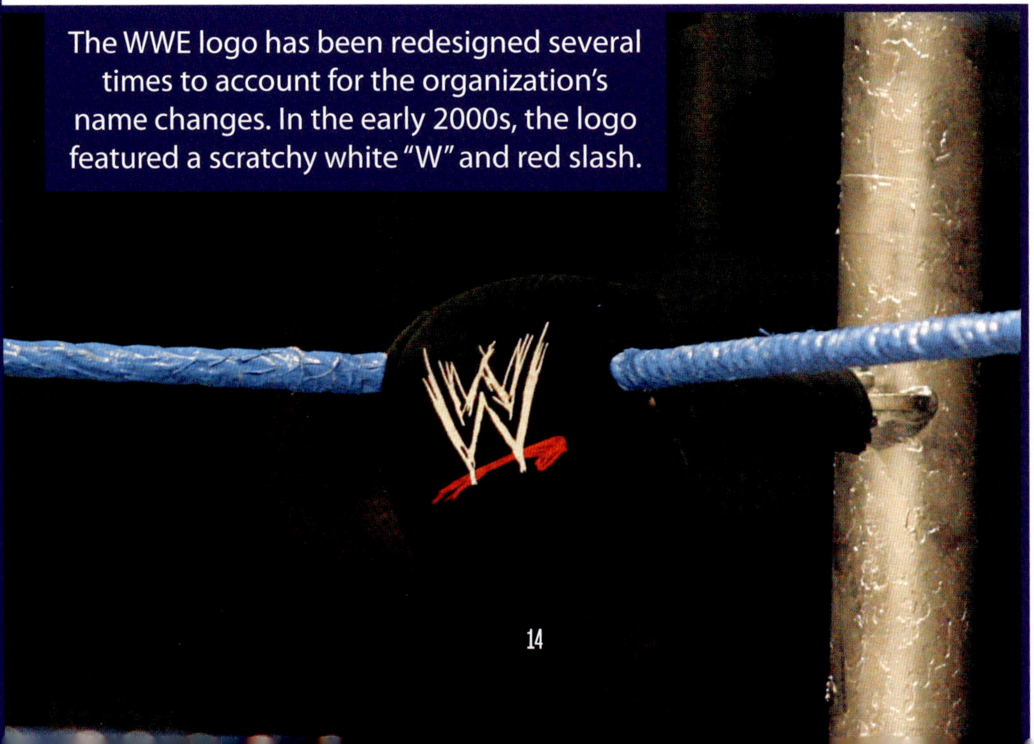

The WWE logo has been redesigned several times to account for the organization's name changes. In the early 2000s, the logo featured a scratchy white "W" and red slash.

such as joining men at matches as their "managers" or sidekicks. During the 1950s, female wrestlers such as the Fabulous Moolah competed. But by 2000, more female wrestlers came into the spotlight. Popular stars such as Chyna emerged, showing that female wrestlers could star in storylines and gain large fan bases.

Still, female wrestlers struggled throughout the decade. To attract audiences, promoters often wanted female wrestlers to wear swimsuits and evening gowns, putting the focus on their looks instead of their athleticism. This changed soon after popular wrestler Trish Stratus retired in 2006. WWE began putting more focus on female wrestlers' strength. It also established new women's competitions, such as the Divas Championship in 2008.

Chyna, *left*, was known for her muscular build and intimidating presence in the ring. She is often credited with paving the way for women in modern pro wrestling.

Cody Rhodes, *left*, faces off against Rey Mysterio, *right*, during WrestleMania XXVII in 2011. The event took place at the Georgia Dome in Atlanta, Georgia.

2010–2020s

Throughout the 2010s, WWE continued to dominate the world of pro wrestling. While WWE lost some top talent over the years, it still soared in popularity. It secured major television deals and hosted huge WrestleMania shows. It also created new reality TV programs, increased its PPV offerings, and kept selling merchandise and attracting new fans. This allowed it to keep making money and remain a dominant force in the wrestling world.

Eventually, in 2019, a new organization emerged to compete with WWE. Jacksonville Jaguars owners Tony Khan and his father, Shahid Khan, founded All Elite Wrestling (AEW). It debuted on May 25, 2019, featuring famous wrestlers Chris Jericho and Maxwell Jacob Friedman, also known as MJF. The organization also signed a major television deal with TNT.

In 2019, AEW launched its own TV series with a signature weekly show to try to compete with WWE. The show featured new wrestlers and characters. Despite AEW's efforts, it was unable to take down WWE's popularity.

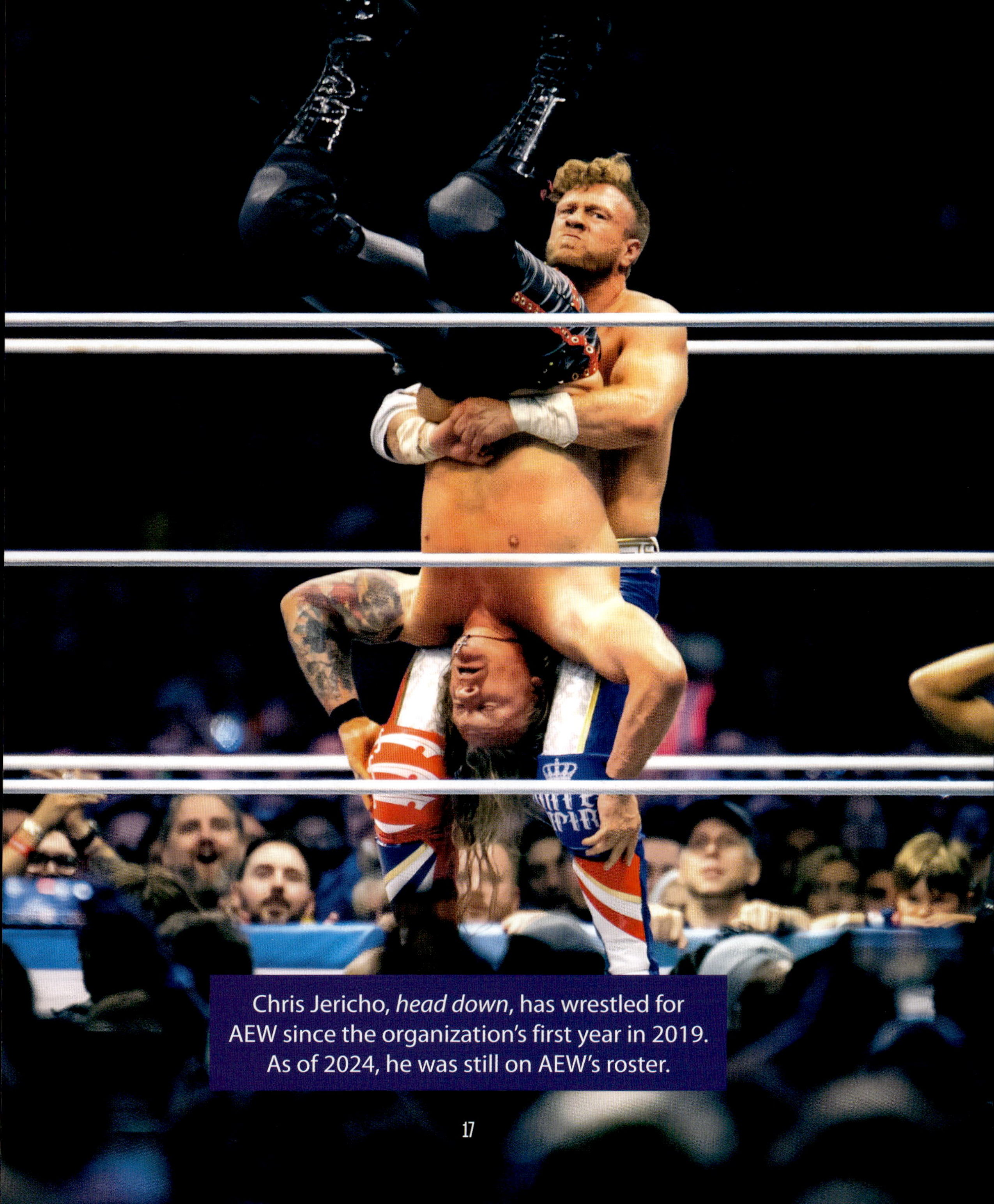

Chris Jericho, *head down*, has wrestled for AEW since the organization's first year in 2019. As of 2024, he was still on AEW's roster.

WRESTLING AROUND THE WORLD

While pro wrestling blossomed in North America, it also developed loyal followings elsewhere. Japan and Mexico have particularly rich histories. These countries have deeply influenced North American wrestling, and vice versa.

JAPAN

In Japan, professional wrestling is called *puroresu*. It began after World War II (1939–1945) but didn't become widely popular until the 1960s and 1970s. Korean-born sumo wrestler Rikidōzan helped turn pro wrestling into a popular sport. In sumo wrestling, competitors try to force opponents out of a circle or make them touch the mat with anything other than their feet. Rikidōzan started the Japan Pro Wrestling Alliance (JWA). He modeled it after US wrestling organizations.

Rikidōzan, *right*, founded the JWA in 1953. He became a pro-wrestling icon throughout Japan and helped recruit talented competitors.

Women's wrestling was also popular in Japan. The All Japan Women's Pro-Wrestling Association was founded in 1955 and became the All Japan

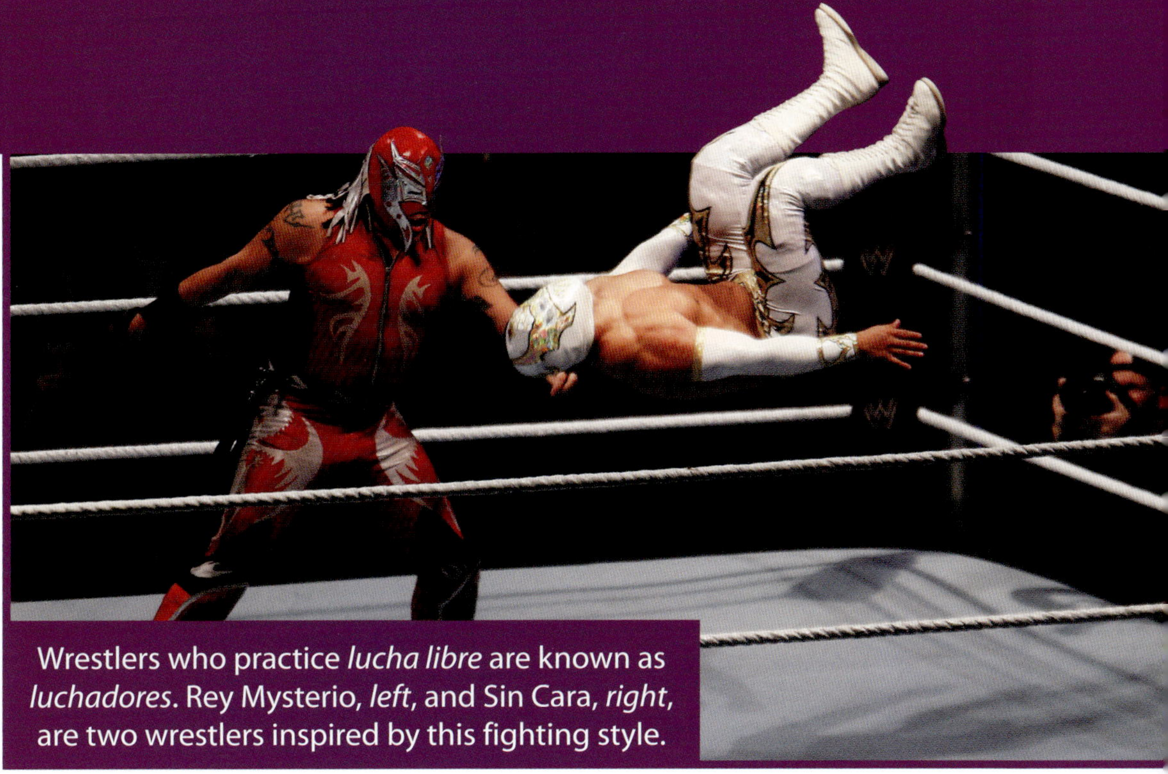

Wrestlers who practice *lucha libre* are known as *luchadores*. Rey Mysterio, *left*, and Sin Cara, *right*, are two wrestlers inspired by this fighting style.

Women's Pro-Wrestling Corporation in 1967. Wrestlers in the organization often competed against wrestlers from other countries. The organization shut down in 2005. Japanese wrestlers who have appeared in WWE include Tatsumi Fujinami, Aja Kong, Shinsuke Nakamura, and Antonio Inoki.

MEXICO

In Mexico, professional wrestlers use a style called *lucha libre*. It features masked heroes, colorful costumes, and aerial maneuvers. It started in the mid-1800s and became popular in the 1930s and 1940s. *Lucha libre* spread across the United States in the 2000s. It has influenced many wrestling performances. Its crisp, colorful style appears in modern US wrestling events. Mexican wrestlers in WWE include Rey Mysterio and Eddie Guerrero.

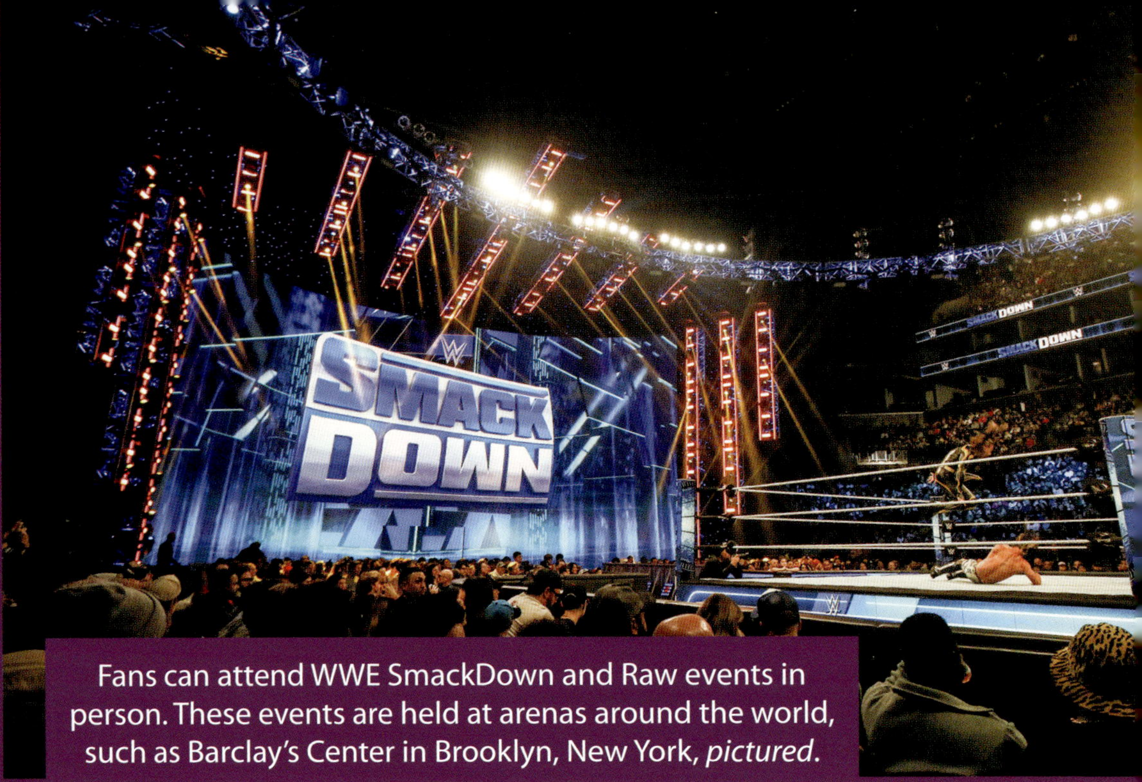

Fans can attend WWE SmackDown and Raw events in person. These events are held at arenas around the world, such as Barclay's Center in Brooklyn, New York, *pictured*.

WWE TODAY

Today, WWE is the world's largest pro-wrestling promotion. It is split into three divisions, or touring brands. Wrestlers in WWE are assigned to compete in shows within a specific division. The WWE's two main divisions, established in 2002, are Raw and SmackDown. Each follows a schedule of events and TV shows. Raw wrestlers appear on the weekly TV program *Monday Night Raw*, while SmackDown wrestlers appear on *Friday Night SmackDown*.

Each brand involves different scripted storylines and has a different roster of competitors. Raw and SmackDown wrestlers usually compete only within their divisions. But they come together for major PPV events such as WrestleMania. Sometimes, wrestlers from one brand also appear in the other brand's shows. Storylines occasionally overlap the brands.

TITLE BELTS

WWE and other wrestling organizations award championship winners with title belts. These are large belts with intricate designs, often made of metal and leather. Winning a title belt is a major accomplishment for pro wrestlers. Different tournaments offer different title belts. Major title belts include the WWE Championship, World Heavyweight Championship, and Women's World Championship.

WWE's third division, NXT, was established in 2010. It is a developmental brand, meaning it is designed for trainees and emerging wrestlers to work their way up into the WWE's more advanced divisions. Because NXT features new stars, its matches tend to showcase more wrestling than scripted entertainment.

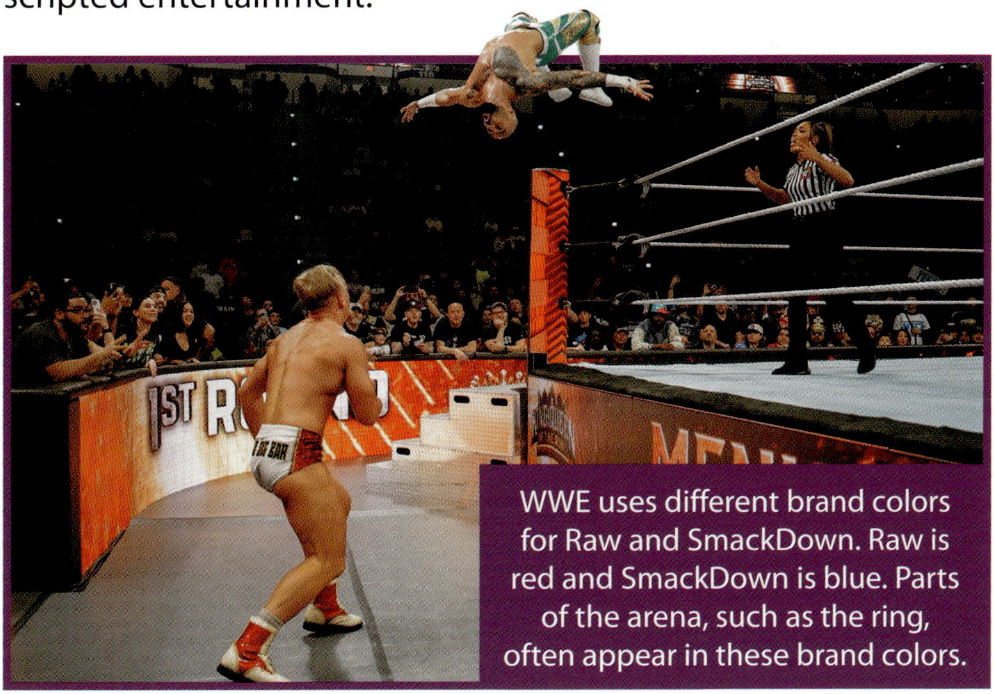

WWE uses different brand colors for Raw and SmackDown. Raw is red and SmackDown is blue. Parts of the arena, such as the ring, often appear in these brand colors.

WRESTLEMANIA

No event in professional wrestling compares to WrestleMania. Since its founding in 1985, WrestleMania has been WWE's signature event each year. The show attracts massive crowds, sometimes topping 100,000 fans. Each year, cities bid to host the event. Fans can attend in person or watch WrestleMania on PPV. They can also watch WrestleMania and other live shows on streaming apps.

The highlight of WrestleMania is typically the last match, or the main event. This is often a WWE championship match. Numerous other matches, in which wrestlers compete for smaller titles, surround the main event. One is the WWE Universal Championship. WrestleMania often features surprise guests, such as celebrities and former wrestlers.

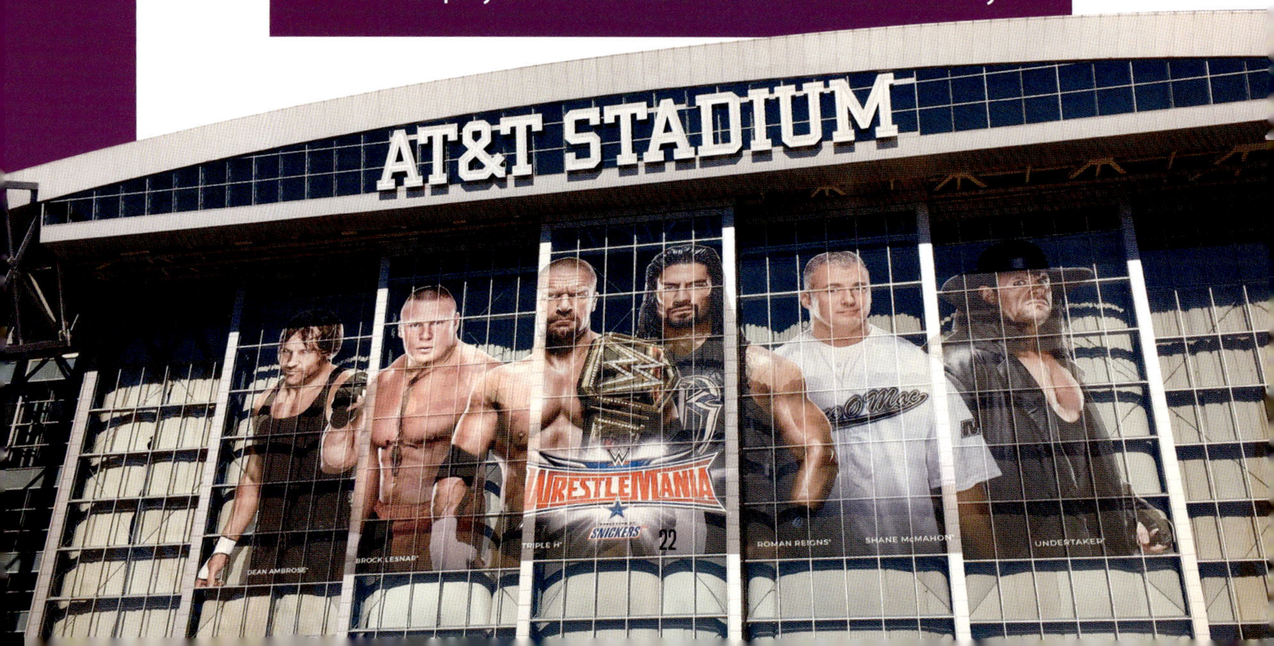

AT&T Stadium in Arlington, Texas, hosted WrestleMania 32 in 2016. Promotional posters and ads for the event were displayed at the stadium and around the city.

In April 2024, WrestleMania XL took place at Lincoln Financial Field in Philadelphia, Pennsylvania. The two-day event featured wrestling stars such as Bayley, *left*.

CELEBRITY MATCHES

WrestleMania often features celebrity matches. Former NFL player Rob Gronkowski appeared at WrestleMania in 2017 and 2020, while former Philadelphia Eagles center Jason Kelce competed in the 2024 WrestleMania XL. Another top celebrity participant was basketball star Shaquille O'Neal, who competed at WrestleMania 32 in 2016.

One of the best fights in the event's history happened during WrestleMania 13 in 1997. Bret Hart and "Stone Cold" Steve Austin performed in a classic "good versus evil" bout that felt like an old-school fight. The match ended with Austin bloodied in the ring, and Hart solidified himself as a villain. Both wrestlers gained fans and fame from the memorable fight, with Austin becoming the face of WWE.

In most tag team matches, teams have an equal number of wrestlers. Partners Asuka, *left*, and Kairi Sane, *right*, have frequently competed in tag team matches as the Kabuki Warriors.

TYPES OF WRESTLING MATCHES

A traditional wrestling match pits two wrestlers against each other. The goal is to pin the opponent for three seconds. In professional wrestling, this is known as a pinfall. A wrestler can win if the opponent submits, or gives up. They can also win if their opponent goes out of the ring for too long.

Pro-wrestling events often feature various types of matches. Tag team matches feature teams of two or more. One wrestler from each team competes in the ring at a time. They can "tag" their teammate to switch places. Ladder matches feature two or more wrestlers in a no-rules fight. They try to get a prize hanging above the ring. They must climb a ladder to reach it.

Other matches are more extreme. Cage matches feature two wrestlers locked in a steel cage. Winners are declared by pinfalls or submissions. Sometimes wrestlers compete to be the first to escape the cage. Cage matches are featured in Hell in a Cell fights and WarGames.

Other individual matches include casket matches, table matches, and no holds barred matches. Casket matches were originally called coffin matches. Competitors try to trap their opponent in a casket. In a table match, wrestlers must throw their opponent through a table. In no holds barred matches, competitors can use weapons and outside resources.

Sammy Guevara, *top*, and Cody Rhodes compete in a 2022 AEW ladder match in Cleveland, Ohio.

INFERNO MATCHES

Inferno matches are one of the most dangerous types of WWE matches. In these matches, the ring is completely surrounded by fire. Competitors try to set their opponents on fire. Only four inferno matches have ever been held. These happened in 1998, 1999, and 2006.

PPV EVENTS

WrestleMania is not the only PPV event. Survivor Series started in 1987. It is the longest-running PPV event after WrestleMania. It features tag team matches in which several wrestlers compete against one another at the same time. In 2022, the event was renamed Survivor Series: WarGames. It featured a type of cage match called a WarGames match. People can watch the event on PPV and streaming apps.

In 1988, WWE started SummerSlam, calling it the Biggest Party of the Summer. The event is held every August. People can view it on streaming apps and PPV.

Undertaker, *right*, battles Brock Lesnar during the main event of SummerSlam 2015. Undertaker went on to win the match.

In January 1988, wrestlers competed in the Royal Rumble at Nassau Coliseum in Uniondale, New York.

Royal Rumble also began in 1988. It is a lead-up event to WrestleMania and one of the most popular PPV events. Wrestlers enter the ring in timed intervals. They try to eliminate opponents by throwing them out of the ring. The last person remaining qualifies for WrestleMania and a spot in the world title match.

Created in 1997, Hell in a Cell is a PPV event that ends with a cage match. Wrestlers compete in a 20-foot (6 m), five-sided steel cage. They can win with a pinfall or by submission.

Another PPV event, Money in the Bank, began in 2005. To win, competitors had to climb a ladder and get a briefcase above the ring. The concept was so popular that it became a regular event.

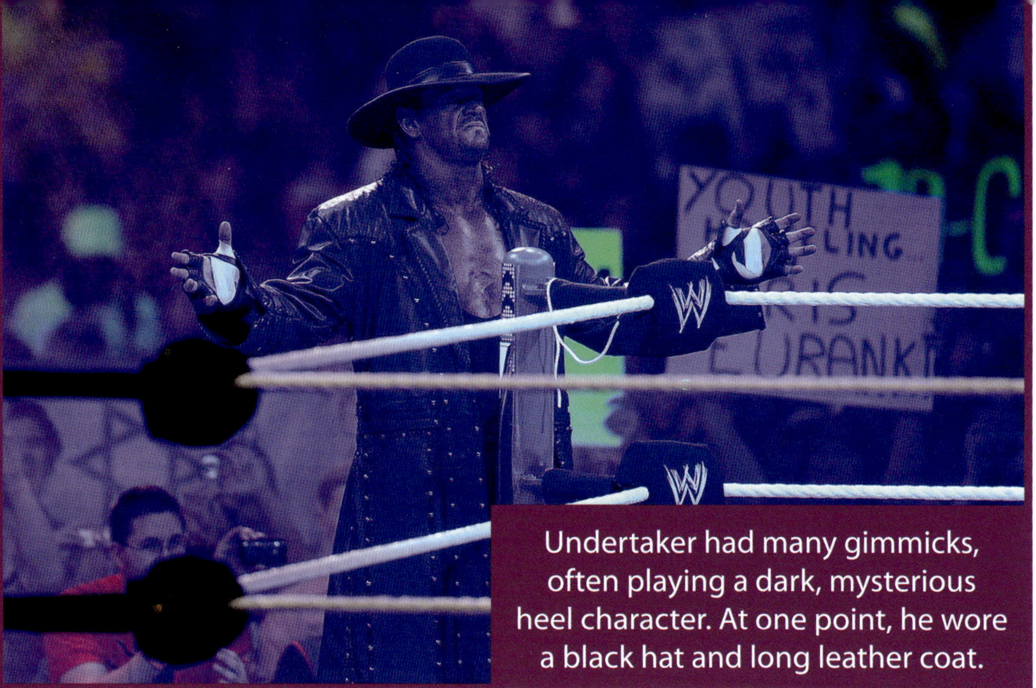

Undertaker had many gimmicks, often playing a dark, mysterious heel character. At one point, he wore a black hat and long leather coat.

COMMON GIMMICKS AND TERMS

Pro wrestling is about more than just fighting. To keep fans entertained, wrestlers tell stories that play out over several weeks or even years. The building blocks of these stories are gimmicks.

Gimmicks are personalities that wrestlers portray during matches. This can include their costume, behavior, and other actions that make them a recognizable character. In wrestling, crowd favorites or heroes are known as babyfaces. Villains are called heels. But gimmicks can go much deeper. For example, Undertaker was at various times a mortician, The Deadman, and a biker.

John Cena started his career as "The Prototype," a robot character. He eventually became the Doctor of Thuganomics. Triple H used numerous gimmicks as a pro wrestler. He was a Chief Operating Officer, the "King of Kings," "The Authority," and "The Game."

WRESTLING TERMS

There are many terms involved in pro wrestling. A wrestler's angle, for example, refers to their character's storyline. Feuds are staged rivalries between wrestlers. A stable is a group of wrestlers who join forces and work together as a team.

There are also many fighting styles. Acrobats spring off the ropes of the ring and fly high into the air. Grapplers focus on wrestling techniques such as pins and submissions. Brawlers focus on moves that require strength and combine strikes and grappling. Big men use their size to defeat and intimidate opponents.

One famous feud in the pro-wrestling world was a rivalry between The Rock, *left*, and Triple H, *right*.

ANDRÉ THE GIANT

André René Roussimoff, known as André the Giant, was born in France in 1946. He had acromegaly. This condition occurs when a person's body produces too much growth hormone, causing them to become unusually tall. By the time André was 12, he was more than six feet (1.8 m) tall and weighed about 200 pounds (91 kg). Eventually he grew to become seven feet, four inches (2.2 m) tall and weigh more than 500 pounds (227 kg). This made him one of the largest pro wrestlers of all time.

When he first started wrestling, André the Giant was nicknamed "Monster Eiffel Tower" and "Monster Roussimoff." In the 1970s and 1980s, he wrestled for several organizations.

André the Giant started wrestling around age 18. His pro-wrestling career began in France in 1966. In the early 1970s, he wrestled in Japan and Canada.

In 1973, André the Giant joined WWWF. Nicknamed the Eighth Wonder of the World, he performed on the pro-wrestling circuit

In 1988, André the Giant and rival Hulk Hogan attended a press conference in New York City to promote "The Main Event," an upcoming match. André went on to defeat Hogan.

FUN FACT

André the Giant portrayed Fezzik, a giant, in the 1987 film *The Princess Bride*.

with the organization for 20 years. He remained undefeated for almost 15 years and had rivalries with Ernie "Big Cat" Ladd, Blackjack Mulligan, and Hulk Hogan. André died in 1993. After his death, he became the first person inducted into the WWE Hall of Fame.

Kurt Angle celebrates after winning a gold medal at the 1996 Olympics. He competed in the freestyle heavyweight category, defeating Iranian wrestler Abbas Jadidi in the final round.

KURT ANGLE

Kurt Angle first rose to fame on a traditional wrestling mat. In 1996, he won an Olympic gold medal while competing for Team USA. He accomplished that while competing with a broken neck. In 1998, he joined WWE.

In the ring, Angle was not quite the tough-guy Olympian. Instead, he was nerdy. He drank milk and his values were the "Three I's"—intensity, integrity, and intelligence. This was funny because Angle cheated to win matches. He also accused other wrestlers of cheating if they defeated him.

Angle used his cleverness to become one of the top pro wrestlers. He was named King of the Ring in 2000.

That same year, Angle defeated The Rock to win his first WWE Championship. He won three more championship titles during his career.

Angle had many rivals in WWE. They included "Stone Cold" Steve Austin, Shawn Michaels, The Rock, Undertaker, Triple H, Big Show, and John Cena. Angle was inducted into the WWE Hall of Fame in 2017.

FUN FACT

Kurt Angle initially turned down an offer to join WWE after the 1996 Olympics.

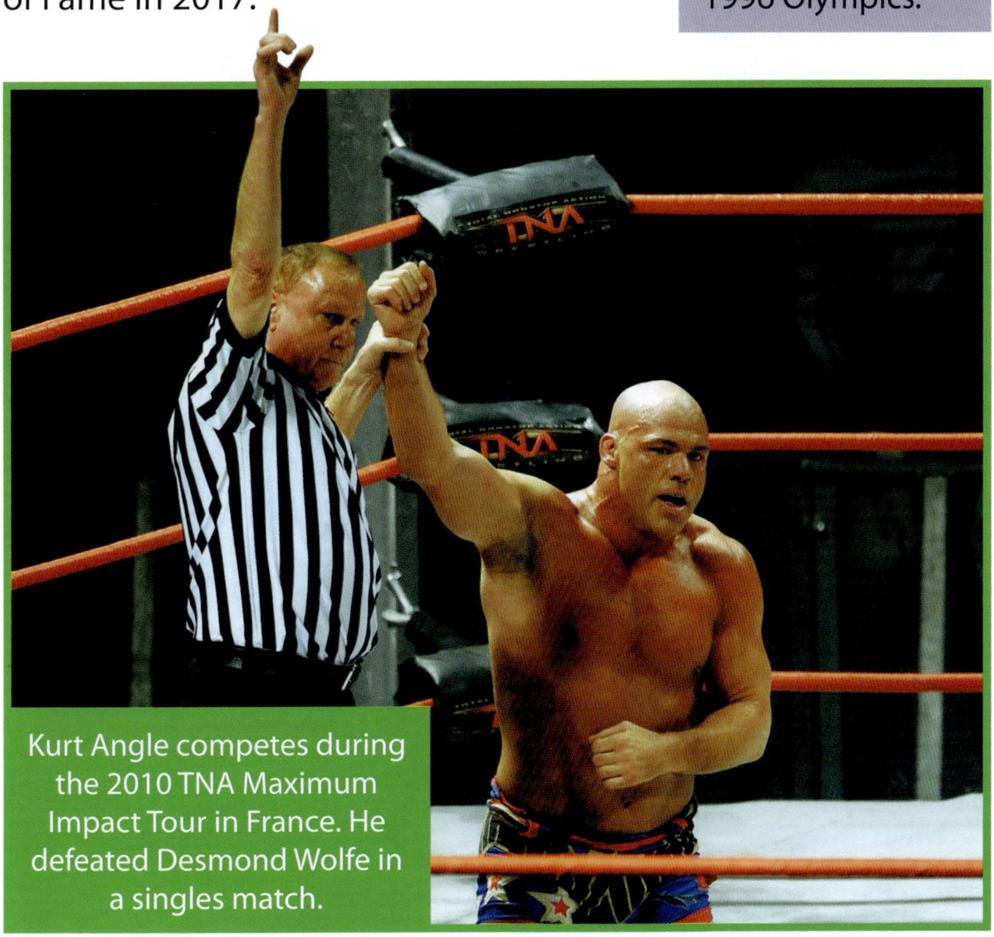

Kurt Angle competes during the 2010 TNA Maximum Impact Tour in France. He defeated Desmond Wolfe in a singles match.

ASUKA

Known as "The Empress," Asuka is considered one of the most successful female WWE wrestlers of all time. She debuted at NXT in October 2015. The Japanese wrestler is known for her signature mask, which is painted on her face. Her mask designs are based on traditional Japanese Noh masks.

When she enters the ring with her mask and colorful battle gear, Asuka shows she's there to win. If her appearance doesn't intimidate her opponent, then her fierce moves will. She uses skilled techniques and an aggressive style

Asuka, *right*, faces off against Shayna Baszler during a *Monday Night Raw* tag team match in March 2024.

Asuka's wrestling costume has changed several times throughout her career. At one point, she appeared in the ring with rainbow hair, a robe, and a single black line painted across her face.

to defeat competitors. In fact, between her debut and WrestleMania 34 in 2018, Asuka did not lose a single time.

Asuka has an impressive pro-wrestling resume. Some highlights include winning the NXT, Raw, and SmackDown women's championships. At the 2023 WWE Elimination Chamber event, Asuka became the first woman to win the Royal Rumble, Money in the Bank, and Elimination Chamber matches.

FUN FACT

Asuka's signature move is the Asuka Lock. She wraps her legs around her opponent's body, holds one of their arms behind their back, and then wraps her arms around the opponent's neck.

"Stone Cold" Steve Austin appeared as a special guest referee during WrestleMania 23 in 2007.

STEVE AUSTIN

When WWE fans heard the sound of shattering glass in the arena, they knew it meant "Stone Cold" Steve Austin was coming. Austin played the part of the everyday man, wearing jeans and drinking beer in the ring. He was considered one of the edgiest pro wrestlers in the WWE Attitude Era. This era lasted from the late 1990s to the early 2000s. During this time, the WWE began focusing on shocking, controversial content that appealed to young adults.

FUN FACT

While with WCW, Austin went by the name "Stunning" Steve Austin.

Austin gladly played the part of the villain, taunting his opponents and doing whatever it took to get to the top. He was aggressive but also successful. He earned many titles, becoming one of the most popular pro wrestlers.

During his career, Austin won six WWE Championships, two Intercontinental Championships, and a record three Royal Rumble events. He was inducted into the WWE Hall of Fame in 2009. Some of his most memorable battles were against The Rock and Vince McMahon.

"Stone Cold" Steve Austin, *left*, had a famous feud with former WWE chairman Vince McMahon, *right*. In 2005, the rivals appeared at a press conference together.

SASHA BANKS (MERCEDES MONÉ)

Known as "The Boss," Sasha Banks is a natural leader and defiant wrestler. She made her debut in 2012 through WWE NXT, a TV show featuring the next generation of WWE stars. She quickly rose to fame and was promoted to the WWE Raw roster in 2015.

Banks made history by competing in the first-ever Women's WWE Iron Man, Hell in a Cell, Royal Rumble, and Elimination Chamber matches. Banks was a member of the Four Horsewomen stable too. She teamed up with Four

Sasha Banks, *top*, battles Nia Jax during the 2017 WWE Live Tour in Lille, France.

In 2023, Banks debuted her new look as Mercedes Moné at the NJPW Wrestle Kingdom 17 event.

> **FUN FACT**
> Sasha Banks is married to former pro wrestler Sarath Ton.

Horsewomen member Bayley to become the first WWE Women's Tag Team Champion in 2019.

Banks won five Raw Women's Titles before leaving WWE in 2022. In 2023, she made her debut with New Japan Pro-Wrestling (NJPW). She took on the ring name Mercedes Moné.

Batista, who stands over six feet (1.8 m) tall, competed in both Raw and SmackDown.

BATISTA

Batista, also known as "The Animal," was a WWE beast who was tough to tame. He started his pro-wrestling career as a goofball in the ring, but he quickly became known for his strength, temper, and fierce moves. He went on to become a four-time world heavyweight champion and two-time WWE Championship winner.

Before Batista competed for pro-wrestling titles, he overcame a troubled childhood in Washington, DC. He was estranged from his parents when he was 17 years old and faced assault charges when he got into a fight at a club. These struggles motivated him to become a professional wrestler.

Batista joined WWE after competing on an independent circuit. He won his first world championship at WrestleMania 21 in 2005, defeating Triple H. Batista held the title for a record 282 days. He also won two Royal Rumbles. Batista left WWE in 2010 but returned in 2014. He retired from wrestling in 2019.

FUN FACT

Dave Bautista, who played Batista, also has a career as an actor. He has played parts in many movies, including *Dune* and *Blade Runner 2049*.

Dave Bautista appeared as Drax in all three *Guardians of the Galaxy* films. It took the hair and makeup team five hours every day to transform Bautista into the character.

BAYLEY

Bayley wanted to be a pro wrestler from a young age. She made her NXT debut in 2012. When she moved up the ranks, her excitement to compete could be felt by both fans and competitors. Sporting a side ponytail, bright clothes, and a constant smile, Bayley was known for warmly interacting with fans and other wrestlers. She was nicknamed the Hugger.

Bayley joined WWE's main roster in 2016. She quickly won her first Raw Women's Championship. In 2019, Bayley and Sasha Banks teamed up to win the first WWE Women's Tag Team Championship.

In October 2019, Bayley ditched the Hugger gimmick and became "The Role Model." This new persona was colder and more aggressive. Bayley quickly became one of WWE's

Bayley, *right*, faces off against Sasha Banks during a 2018 WWE match. The two wrestlers often competed against each other or worked together as a team.

In 2024, Bayley appeared at the Backlash France event in Lyon, France. She successfully defended her WWE Women's Championship title.

FUN FACT

Bayley outlasted 29 wrestlers to win the 2024 Women's Royal Rumble.

top female villains. She won the SmackDown Women's Championship in 2019. Bayley also teamed up with Dakota Kai and IYO SKY to form the stable Damage CTRL in 2022.

Bianca Belair jumps over her opponent Carmella during *Monday Night Raw* in 2023. Belair defeated Carmella in the match.

BIANCA BELAIR

Bianca Belair considers herself "The EST." This stands for strong*est*, fast*est*, tough*est*, and b*est*. A fierce competitor, she often uses her long braid to whip her opponents.

Belair debuted in NXT in 2016. In 2017, she deadlifted 415 pounds (188 kg) to top the field at the NXT Combine, an event that tests wrestlers' athletic abilities. A deadlift involves lifting a heavy weight from a standing position without using equipment or a bench.

FUN FACT

Before becoming a pro wrestler, Belair was an All-American track star at the University of Tennessee.

Belair made her WWE debut at WrestleMania 36 in 2020, helping the Street Profits tag team. Belair moved to the main roster, competing in both Raw and SmackDown. In 2021, she won the Royal Rumble Match and defeated Sasha Banks at WrestleMania 37 to win the SmackDown Women's Title.

In 2021, Belair was selected by Raw in the first round of the 2021 WWE Draft. She defeated Big Time Becks to win the Raw Women's Title at Showcase of the Immortals. She was later selected to join SmackDown.

Belair often poses holding her famous hair braid. In 2021, she posed with her braid and title belt during a wrestling event at the Rolling Loud Miami hip-hop festival in Florida.

Big Show lifts CM Punk during the main event of the WWE Tribute to the Troops holiday special in 2011.

BIG SHOW

Big Show, whose real name is Paul Wight, was known for his large size. Like André the Giant, he suffered from acromegaly, which caused him to grow abnormally large. The pro wrestler weighed 383 pounds (174 kg) and wore a size 22 EEEEE shoe. In the 1990s, he had surgery to correct the condition and halt his growth.

In 2008, Big Show appeared at a WrestleMania XXIV press conference in New York City.

Nicknamed "The World's Largest Athlete," Big Show stormed onto the scene in 1995 when he defeated Hulk Hogan to win the WCW World Championship. He joined WWE in 1999 and won numerous titles. He was the first wrestler to win the WWE, WCW, and ECW championships. He competed in several memorable clashes during his career. He battled another large wrestler, Brock Lesnar, in 2003. The ring collapsed due to the size of the two wrestlers. Because of his size, Lesnar was one of Big Show's main rivals. In 2008, Big Show knocked out Undertaker.

FUN FACT

Big Show appeared in the 1998 film *The Waterboy*. He played the role of Captain Insano.

Former Bloodline members Jey Uso, *top*, and Jimmy Uso, *bottom*, faced off against each other at WrestleMania XL in 2024. Jey won the match.

THE BLOODLINE

The Bloodline is one of the most dominant stables in the pro-wrestling world. The villainous stable formed on SmackDown in 2021. Before the group formed, twin brothers Jey and Jimmy Uso, who competed as the tag team The Usos, had a feud with Roman Reigns and the Shield stable. After Reigns left the Shield, he eventually joined forces with the Usos as the leader, or "Tribal Chief," of the Bloodline. Paul Heyman served as the stable's manager.

The Usos and Reigns all went on to claim multiple WWE championships and tag team titles. Solo Sikoa, the younger brother of The Usos, joined the Bloodline in 2022. The same year, Sami Zayn became an honorary member of the group. Most of the Bloodline's past and present members, including Reigns, The Usos, and The Rock, are part of the Anoa'i family.

The group's storylines often feature feuds between stable members. At SummerSlam 2023, for example, Jimmy Uso betrayed Jey Uso in a shocking match. The brothers went on to battle each other at WrestleMania XL in 2024. That year, Tama Tonga and Tanga Loa joined the Bloodline.

FUN FACT

Roman Reigns is Jimmy and Jey Uso's first cousin, once removed.

Bloodline members Tama Tonga, Solo Sikoa, Tango Loa, and Paul Heyman, *left to right*, raise their fingers after winning a 2024 match. The stable is known for using the gesture.

Booker T, *seated*, faces off against La Resistance during a WrestleMania XX tag team match.

BOOKER T

Booker T played many roles as a pro wrestler. Before joining WCW in 1993, he wrestled on smaller circuits as the character G.I. Bro, a soldier. For most of his WWE career, Booker T played the role of a hero. His biggest rivals during this time were Christian, Triple H, and Kurt Angle.

FUN FACT

Booker T met his wife, Sharmell Huffman, when she was a member of the WCW's dance group, the Nitro Girls.

Booker T won the WCW Tag Team Championship 11 times and the World Championship six times. After winning the 2006 King of the Ring event, he began wrestling as King Booker. He wore a crown and spoke with a British accent.

After he retired in 2012, Booker T became a commentator for WWE's SmackDown. He also appeared as a trainer on the reality show *WWE Tough Enough* and served as general manager of SmackDown. In addition, Booker T founded his own wrestling school, the Reality of Wrestling. He was inducted into the WWE Hall of Fame in 2013.

Booker T and his wife, Sharmell, attended a charity event in 2018. Sharmell wrestled alongside her husband as the character Queen Sharmell.

DANIEL BRYAN

Daniel Bryan was seen as a WWE underdog. The determined wrestler frequently clashed with the McMahon family and the Authority stable. The Authority had formed to help Randy Orton defeat Bryan and win the WWE Championship at the 2013 SummerSlam.

Bryan stood up to the Authority. Every time they tried to take him down, Bryan fought back. However, the odds were always against him.

In 2014, Daniel Bryan entered the ring at WrestleMania XXX wearing a "Yes!" movement T-shirt.

Daniel Bryan celebrates after winning the WWE World Heavyweight Championship at WrestleMania XXX, which took place at the Mercedes-Benz Superdome in New Orleans, Louisiana.

This made Bryan a fan favorite. WWE fans campaigned to get Bryan into the main event of WrestleMania XXX in 2014. Since Bryan's signature chant was "Yes! Yes! Yes!," his fans called their campaign the "Yes!" Movement. Their efforts paid off, and Bryan defeated Randy Orton and Batista to claim the WWE World Heavyweight Championship.

Bryan won a WWE championship, WWE Tag Team Championship, and SmackDown Tag Team Championship. He was also a Money in the Bank winner. Bryan was a Grand Slam Champion and holds the record for the longest amount of time in a Royal Rumble Match. He left WWE in 2021 and joined AEW. As of 2024, he was competing as Bryan Danielson.

FUN FACT

Daniel Bryan was influenced by mixed martial arts (MMA), but never pursued an MMA career.

Former Bullet Club members Karl Anderson, *left*, and Prince Devitt, *right*, compete against each other in 2017. Devitt, the stable's original leader, later changed his ring name to Finn Bálor.

THE BULLET CLUB

The popular Bullet Club stable formed in 2013. Fergal Devitt, also known as Prince Devitt, originally led the group of villains. Karl Anderson, Bad Luck Fale, and Tama Tonga were other original members. The group fought in NJPW.

Often compared to the New World Order, the Bullet Club was known for making wrestlers into stars. The group was popular among fans, and those who joined the stable soon became known by fans around the world. As wrestlers moved up to WWE and other organizations, the group's competitors changed. Former members include Kenny Omega and

AJ Styles. The stable's members are known for their confidence, ferocity, and betrayals.

The Bullet Club has won numerous titles. Some of the stable's top titles include four International Wrestling Grand Prix (IWGP) Heavyweight championships and two IWGP Intercontinental championships. The stable has won nine IWGP Tag Team Championships too.

FUN FACT

David Finlay, who took over as Bullet Club leader in 2023, is a fourth-generation wrestler.

David Finlay, *center*, became the Bullet Club's leader during NJPW's 51st anniversary show in 2023.

JOHN CENA

John Cena is considered the public face of the WWE and is one of its most popular pro wrestlers. He originally pursued a career as a bodybuilder before turning to wrestling. A 16-time world champion, Cena has portrayed many memorable characters. Early in his career, Cena wrestled as the Doctor of Thuganomics. He wore sports jerseys and

FUN FACT

John Cena has granted more Make-A-Wish requests than any other athlete in WWE. He has done more than 600 Make-A-Wish visits with kids.

John Cena, *left*, celebrates his victory over The Miz during a *Monday Night Raw* Halloween event in 2011.

John Cena became known for wearing denim shorts or cargo shorts in the ring. He also wore colorful wristbands and armbands.

showcased his love of rapping, which made his matches entertaining and added to his storylines.

After 2005, Cena took on a more family-friendly character. He focused on the values of "hustle, loyalty, and respect" and used his large muscular build to defeat opponents. Cena's fan base, known as "Cenation," embraced his new character and message of "Never give up."

Cena's biggest rivals included The Rock, Randy Orton, Batista, Brock Lesnar, and Triple H. In addition to his success in the ring, Cena has also recorded an album. He has acted in movies too.

Chyna's real name was Joan Laurer. She made her pro-wrestling debut as Chyna in 1997.

CHYNA

Called "The Ninth Wonder of the World," Chyna was a powerful, fierce wrestler with a muscular build. Competing during the Attitude Era, Chyna was an original member of the stable D-Generation X. After serving as a bodyguard to Triple H and Shawn Michaels, Chyna quickly rose to individual fame.

Chyna broke gender barriers for female wrestlers, becoming the first woman to qualify for the King of the Ring tournament and Royal Rumble Match in 1999. She also became the first

FUN FACT

Chyna's name was a play on the ceramic material china, which is very fragile. The name contrasted with Chyna's strength.

woman to win the Intercontinental Championship. She won the WWE Women's Championship at WrestleMania X-Seven in 2001. Chyna paved the way for future female WWE stars, including Lita and Trish Stratus, by showing that they could be muscular and aggressive wrestlers and compete against men. She passed away in 2016.

Chyna and Triple H were a real-life couple for several years and frequently teamed up for WWE matches.

THE DANGEROUS ALLIANCE

The Dangerous Alliance was a pro-wrestling stable formed in 1991 during an episode of *WCW Saturday Night*. Promoter Paul Heyman founded the group. Its members included Rick Rude, Steve Austin, Arn Anderson, Bobby Eaton, Larry Zbyszko, and Madusa.

The group dominated WCW during its reign in the early 1990s. At one point, Rude was the US Champion, Austin was the TV Champion, and Eaton and Anderson were the Tag Team Champions. The only title the group's members didn't hold was the World Heavyweight Championship.

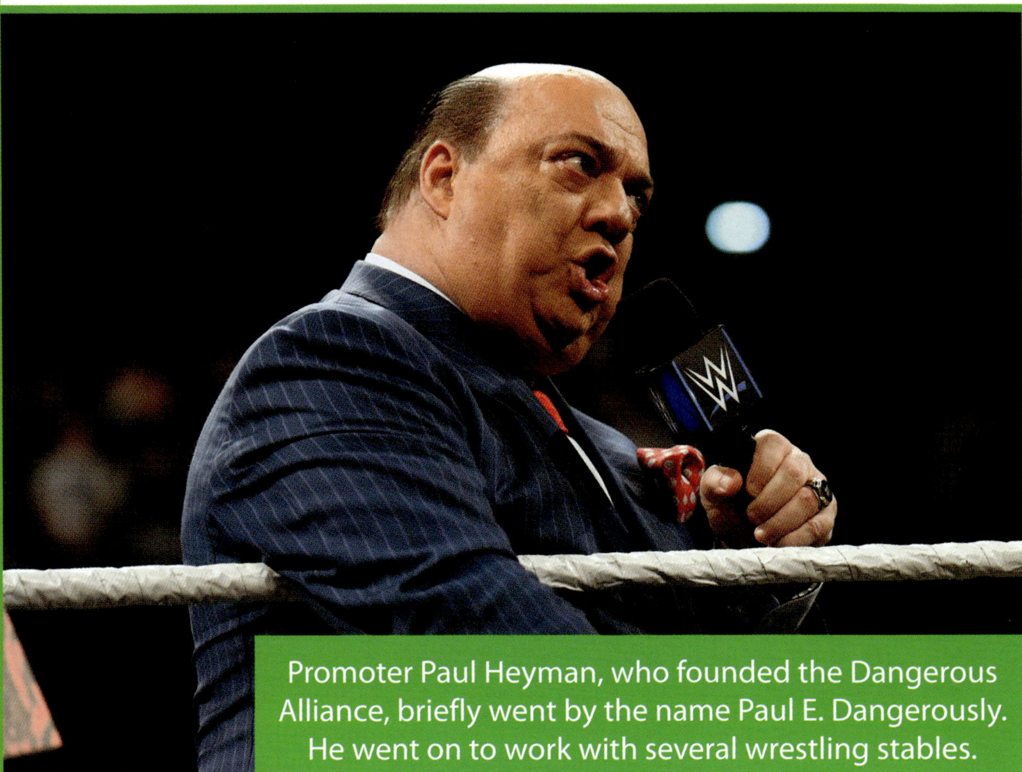

Promoter Paul Heyman, who founded the Dangerous Alliance, briefly went by the name Paul E. Dangerously. He went on to work with several wrestling stables.

Dangerous Alliance member Rick Rude was often called "Ravishing" Rick Rude. His character was known for being arrogant and wearing showy costumes.

> **FUN FACT**
>
> In 1992, the Dangerous Alliance's enemies joined together to form a group called Sting's Squadron.

The Dangerous Alliance lasted for about a year. During this time, its members competed in several memorable matches. In 1992, they lost to the Steiner Brothers in a tag team match. The group's biggest feud was with Sting. He led a group that defeated the Dangerous Alliance in 1992.

D-GENERATION X

D-Generation X, often called DX, was a WWE stable formed in 1997. It featured some of the most popular pro wrestlers, including Triple H, Shawn Michaels, and Chyna. Later, Road Dogg, Billy Gunn, and X-Pac joined the group.

D-Generation X member Shawn Michaels, *front*, reunited with Triple H, *back*, for a tag team match in 2018.

When the group entered the ring, the question "Are you ready?" was announced to the audience. DX members were known for being rebels, breaking the rules, and challenging WWE authorities. They used immature gestures and rude language to gain fans, especially teens. Some of their behavior pushed the limits of what was acceptable to show on television.

> **FUN FACT**
> The members of D-Generation X continue to compete and reunite at special events.

Chyna was the stable's enforcer. This made D-Generation X the first group to feature a woman as an aggressive leader or bodyguard. As DX's popularity rose, Triple H, Chyna, and Michaels became some of the most popular WWE competitors.

Michaels stepped away from the WWE in 1998. After that, the second version of D-Generation X formed. The stable was inducted into the WWE Hall of Fame in 2019.

In 2011, D-Generation X member Shawn Michaels, *second from left*, was inducted into the WWE Hall of Fame. Fellow stable members Triple H, *second from right,* and X-Pac, *right*, attended the induction ceremony.

TED "THE MILLION DOLLAR MAN" DiBIASE

The Million Dollar Man, whose real name is Ted DiBiase, used his money to find success in the WWE. He showed off his wealth and thought he was better than everyone else because of his fortune. During matches, he wore a suit with dollar signs on it and ordered his servant, Virgil, around. He also stuffed $100 bills into the mouths of competitors after defeating them.

When the Million Dollar Man wanted something, he bought it. He "purchased" a spot in the

FUN FACT

The Million Dollar Man's son, also named Ted DiBiase, was a WWE wrestler too.

In 1989, the Million Dollar Man invented the Million Dollar Championship belt. It was made of gold and featured diamond-encrusted dollar signs.

In 2010, the Million Dollar Man, *center*, was inducted into the WWE Hall of Fame. During the induction ceremony, he appeared onstage with his sons Ted DiBiase Jr., *left*, and Brett DiBiase, *right*.

1989 Royal Rumble and even bought a WWE championship from André the Giant. He also created his own wrestling title, the Million Dollar Championship.

The Million Dollar Man is known for adding Undertaker to his 1990 Survivor Series team. Since his debut, Undertaker has become a successful WWE star. The Million Dollar Man was a three-time WWE Tag Team Champion and was inducted into the WWE Hall of Fame in 2010.

Edge interacts with the crowd before a match at WrestleMania XXVII. He went on to defeat Alberto Del Rio.

EDGE

Edge was the rock star of the WWE. During the 1990s and 2000s, he became known for his big hair, leather jackets, and rock star poses. His large group of fans called themselves Edgeheads.

In school, Adam Copeland, who portrayed Edge, was voted "Most Likely to Be WWE Champion." But his path to the WWE was a long one. Edge worked factory jobs to make money and help his single mother. At age 18, he won an essay contest to earn free wrestling lessons.

Edge competed in independent organizations throughout the 1990s before signing a WWE contract in 1997. He formed a tag team with Christian, and the pair won seven championships together. Edge also excelled at singles matches, winning 31 titles. He retired in 2011 after suffering a serious injury. However, he returned to the ring in 2020 at the Royal Rumble.

FUN FACT

Edge is a fan of the rock band KISS and has a large guitar collection.

Edge, *top*, battles Finn Bálor during the WWE Clash at the Castle event in 2022.

EVOLUTION

Evolution was a WWE stable that had a huge impact on the organization between 2003 and 2005. The group of villains represented the past, present, and future of the WWE. Legendary pro wrestler Ric Flair was the past, Triple H was the present, and Randy Orton and Batista were the future. Together, the group was ruthless and successful.

In December 2003, Evolution won Raw's three major championships. These are the World Heavyweight, Intercontinental, and World Tag Team titles. The group's members were all popular, and being in Evolution made them

Evolution members Randy Orton, Batista, and Ric Flair, *left to right*, appeared at WrestleMania XX in 2004.

The members of Evolution split up in 2005 after Triple H, *pictured*, betrayed Ric Flair. The group reunited in 2014.

even more so. Triple H became one of the top heels in the WWE, while Batista and Orton were top competitors. Flair's presence in the group gave it more credibility since he was an established and well-known wrestler.

FUN FACT

Batista was originally not going to be part of Evolution. Mark Jindrak was supposed to be included in the group instead.

THE FABULOUS FREEBIRDS

The Fabulous Freebirds were the first pro wrestlers to form a tag team of three members. Formed in 1979, the big-haired, flashy group included Michael "P.S." Hayes, Terry "Bam Bam" Gordy, and Buddy "Jack" Roberts. They teamed up to win the NWA Georgia Tag Team Championship, which later became the NWA National Tag Team Championship.

After the stable's victory, the Freebird Rule was implemented. It states that any two-man combination of a group's members could defend a tag team title. This gave teams more options because it meant other wrestlers could compete, instead of only the pair who originally won the title. Numerous groups used this rule, including Demolition and Spirit Squad.

Michael "P. S." Hayes, *right*, served as the leader of The Fabulous Freebirds. The stable formed only two years after Hayes debuted.

FUN FACT

The Fabulous Freebirds used "Badstreet, U.S.A." as their walk-in song during competitions. This started the trend of wrestlers using entrance music.

The Fabulous Freebirds won the Six-Man Tag Team Title six times in World Class Championship Wrestling (WCCW). They also won NWA American Tag Team Titles in 1980 and 1981. They later added a fourth member, Jimmy "Jam" Garvin, and joined WWE as part of Cyndi Lauper's Rock 'n' Wrestling Connection.

Michael "P. S." Hayes, *left*, and Jimmy "Jam" Garvin, *right*, were inducted into the WWE Hall of Fame in 2016.

The Fabulous Moolah competed at WrestleMania 2 in 1986, successfully defending her Women's Championship title.

FABULOUS MOOLAH

Mary Lillian Ellison, better known as the Fabulous Moolah, was the longest reigning champion in women's wrestling. At the start of her career, she was one of wrestling's first female valets. The Fabulous Moolah started competing in the mid-1950s.

In 1956, she won the Battle Royal to claim the Women's Championship of the World. She held the title for 28 years. During her WWE reign, the Fabulous Moolah was the first woman to wrestle in Madison Square Garden in New York City. She lost her title in 1984 when she was defeated by Wendi Richter. The match aired on MTV.

The Fabulous Moolah retired from wrestling in 1987. She became the first woman inducted into the WWE Hall of Fame in 1995. She died in 2007 at the age of 84.

The Fabulous Moolah, *pictured*, trained with women's wrestling champion and promoter Mildred Burke in the 1940s.

FUN FACT

The Fabulous Moolah played the role of the "Queen" of WWE during her final championship, accompanying King Harley Race and manager Bobby Heenan in the ring.

Charlotte Flair holds up her title belt at WrestleMania 39 in 2023. She faced off against Rhea Ripley.

CHARLOTTE FLAIR

Charlotte Flair is the daughter of pro-wrestling legend Ric Flair. With her athletic ability, style, and confidence, she has made a name for herself in the wrestling world. Flair has won more championships than any other woman in WWE history, winning the Divas Championship,

FUN FACT

Charlotte Flair played college volleyball at Appalachian State University in North Carolina.

Raw Women's Championship, and SmackDown Women's Championship.

Flair has gained a large fan following, helping her become the first female WWE wrestler in a main event singles match on Raw, SmackDown, and PPV. There have been many highlights in Flair's wrestling career, including some historical achievements. In 2018, she ended Asuka's undefeated streak at WrestleMania 34. The following year, Flair competed in the WrestleMania 35 main event against Ronda Rousey and Becky Lynch. The trio were the first women to ever headline WrestleMania. Despite her success, Flair wants more. Her goal is to win more world titles than her legendary father.

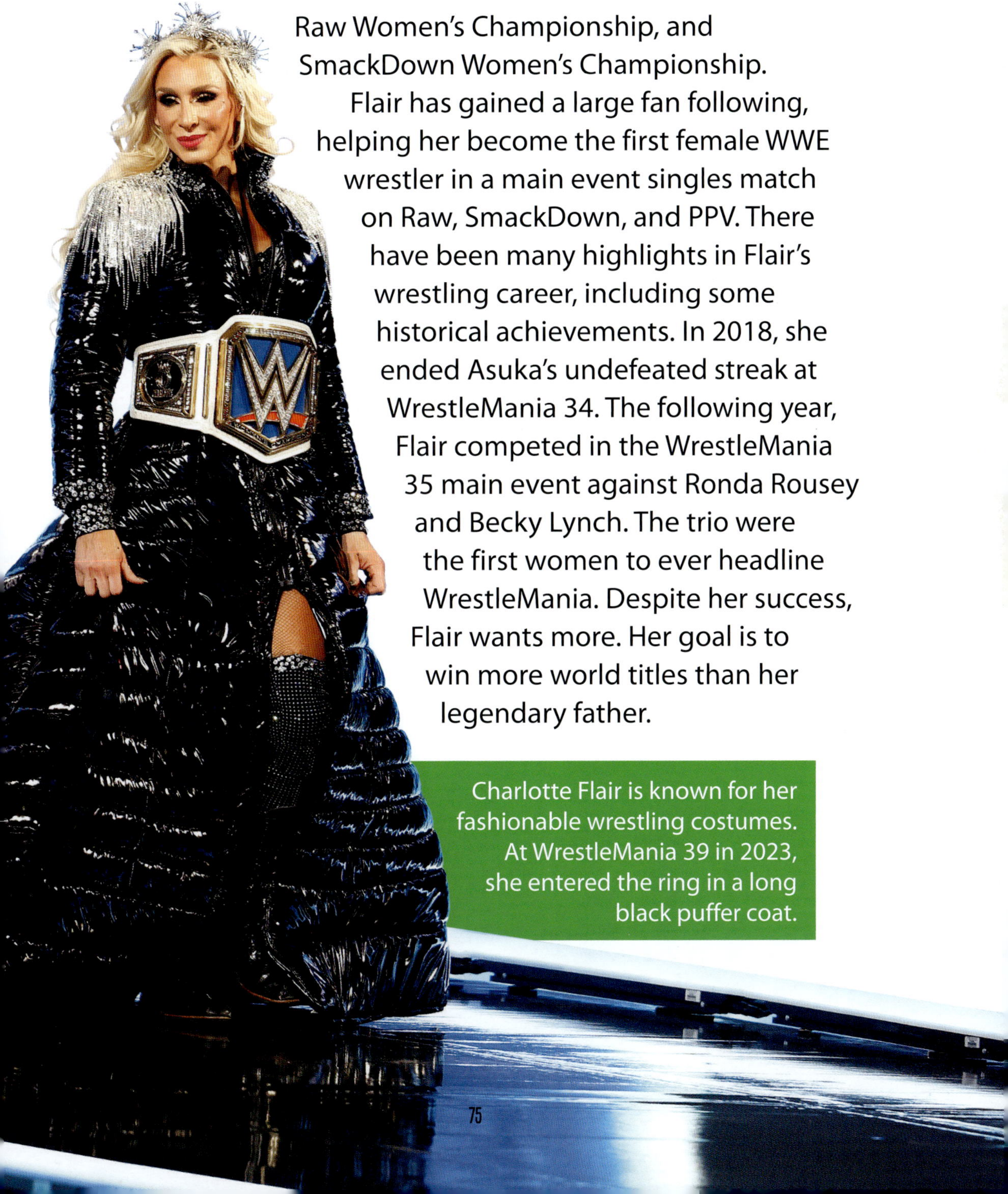

Charlotte Flair is known for her fashionable wrestling costumes. At WrestleMania 39 in 2023, she entered the ring in a long black puffer coat.

RIC FLAIR

Ric Flair had a loud, confident presence in the ring. With his flashy robes, strutting walk, and signature "Wooooo!" yell, Flair was a fan favorite. He was known for his skill and charismatic presence during matches.

After dropping out of college to pursue wrestling, Flair became a 16-time world champion. He trained under legendary wrestler Verne Gagne in 1971. He then competed in the AWA, where he battled against top names such as Dusty Rhodes, André the Giant, and Wahoo McDaniel.

Flair's career derailed in 1975 when he broke his back in a plane crash. He was told he would never wrestle again. But Flair, who competed as "The Nature Boy," returned to the ring six months later to compete in NWA.

Flair made his WWE debut in 1991. In 2008,

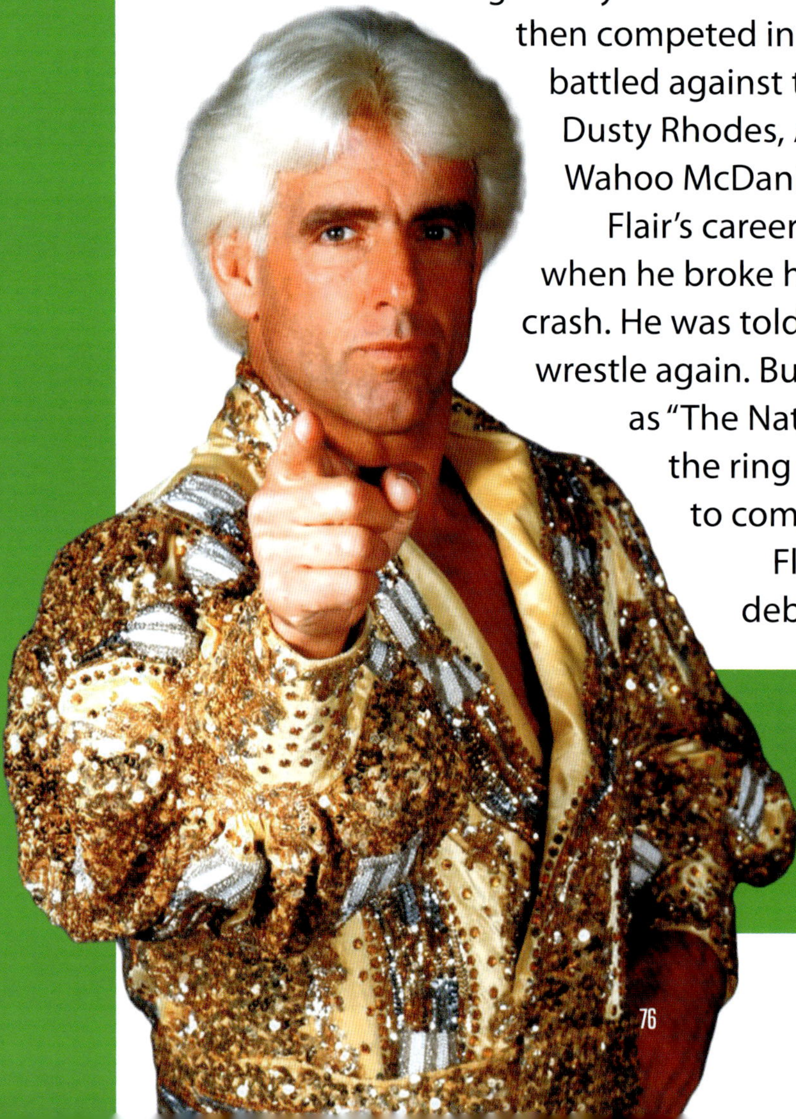

Ric Flair often walked out to the ring wearing fancy robes. Many of his robes featured intricate beading or embroidery.

In 2009, Ric Flair appeared at the Hulkamania Tour in Perth, Australia. He faced off against Hulk Hogan.

FUN FACT

Ric Flair owns a company called Wooooo! Wings. It focuses on chicken wing delivery orders.

he became the first active competitor to be inducted into the WWE Hall of Fame. He later became the first two-time inductee when he was inducted with the Four Horsemen in 2012.

Later in his career, Mick Foley, *second from right*, appeared as a special guest referee in several wrestling matches.

MICK FOLEY

Mick Foley competed under three different personas. These included the ferocious Cactus Jack and the hippie character Dude Love. His third persona was Mankind, a mental patient in a leather mask.

As Cactus Jack, Foley gained fans after surviving serious injuries, including getting an ear torn off and suffering burns in an exploding ring. In 1996, he

FUN FACT

Mick Foley wrote a *New York Times*-bestselling autobiography titled *Have a Nice Day: A Tale of Blood and Sweatsocks*.

became Mankind. As Mankind, Foley survived a career-defining moment when he was thrown off the top of Hell in a Cell by Undertaker.

Foley retired in 2000 but returned to WWE as a commissioner and commentator. He also occasionally returned to the ring, most notably at WrestleMania 22, where he competed against Edge. Foley was inducted into the WWE Hall of Fame in 2013.

In 2023, Mick Foley appeared at Motor City Comic Con in Novi, Michigan.

THE FOUR HORSEMEN

The Four Horsemen formed in 1986. Despite its name, the stable had five members. It originally included Ric Flair, Arn Anderson, Tully Blanchard, Barry Windham, and JJ Dillon. Numerous other wrestlers also competed in the group, including Dean Malenko and Curt Hennig.

The stable took professional wrestling to a new level. Its members wore expensive suits while other competitors wore

Four Horsemen members Arn Anderson, Ric Flair, and Barry Windham, *left to right*, attended the WWE Hall of Fame induction ceremony in 2012.

In 2019, former Four Horsemen member Arn Anderson appeared at GalaxyCon Raleigh in Raleigh, North Carolina.

cheap attire, and they flew on private jets as part of their storylines. The Four Horsemen also made a statement in the ring. At the 1988 Great American Bash, Anderson, Blanchard, Windham, and Flair all retained their titles.

The Four Horsemen ended when Anderson and Blanchard joined WWF in 1988. But the stable influenced and inspired other groups. Its members have been inducted into the WWE Hall of Fame.

FUN FACT

The Four Horsemen formed during a TV promo. After the group of heels filmed a segment together, they decided to form a stable.

Verne Gagne started his wrestling career as an amateur, winning several state championships during his college years.

VERNE GAGNE

Verne Gagne played a pivotal role in professional wrestling. He founded AWA and was its most successful competitor. As a promoter, he also helped boost pro wrestling's popularity.

Before becoming a legendary professional wrestler, Gagne wrestled and played football at the University of Minnesota. He also briefly played for the Green Bay Packers football team. He made his pro-wrestling debut in 1960. Gagne competed until the 1980s and eventually became the owner of AWA.

Many wrestlers competed on Gagne's AWA tour, including Jesse "The Body" Ventura, the Legion of Doom, Shawn Michaels, and Marty Jannetty. Gagne's son, Greg, competed too. Gagne also played a role in creating Hulkamania. Hulk Hogan was part of AWA, but he left in 1983 after failing to win any titles. Hogan went to WWE and became one of pro wrestling's most popular entertainers.

As a professional wrestler, Gagne won the AWA Championship ten times between 1960 and 1981. He was inducted into the WWE Hall of Fame in 2006.

FUN FACT

Verne Gagne was an alternate for the US wrestling team at the 1948 Olympic Games. But he did not compete in the games.

Verne Gagne, *right*, battles Dutch Hefner during a 1952 match.

GOLDBERG

Goldberg, nicknamed "Da Man," was a forceful pro-wrestling competitor. A former defensive tackle in the National Football League (NFL), Goldberg was big and athletic. He quickly made his mark on the pro-wrestling circuit. Within a year

FUN FACT

After joining WWE, Goldberg got into a backstage fight with Chris Jericho. The two wrestlers got past it and became good friends.

Before dominating WWE as a wrestler, Goldberg played football for the University of Georgia and for the Atlanta Falcons NFL team.

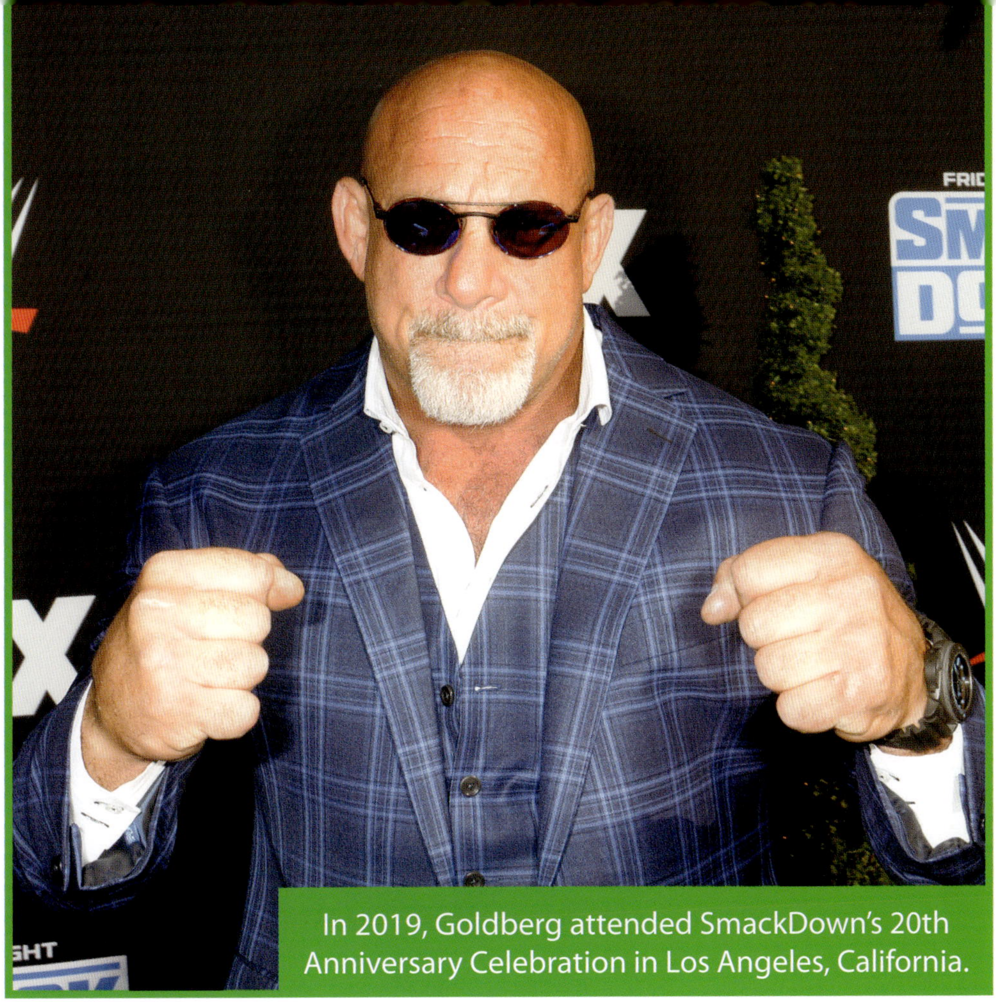

In 2019, Goldberg attended SmackDown's 20th Anniversary Celebration in Los Angeles, California.

of his debut, Goldberg defeated Hulk Hogan to win the WCW World Heavyweight Championship in 1998.

Goldberg had two signature moves, the Spear and the Jackhammer. He remained undefeated from September 1997 to December 1998, earning a 173–0 record. During this stretch, he defeated top competitors such as Big Show and Curt Hennig. Goldberg's streak ended when he lost to Kevin Nash.

Goldberg wrestled for All Japan Pro Wrestling (AJPW) from 2002 to 2003. He later wrestled for WWE. He earned four world championship titles between WCW and WWE. He was inducted into the WWE Hall of Fame in 2018.

Eddie Guerrero leaps from the ropes while competing at WrestleMania XX. He defeated Kurt Angle to retain the WWE Championship title.

EDDIE GUERRERO

Eddie Guerrero, the son of a wrestling promoter, was introduced to wrestling as a child. He wrestled during college and later wrestled in Mexico and Japan. He joined ECW in 1995. He made an instant splash in his first year, winning

FUN FACT

Eddie Guerrero's signature moves were the Frog Splash, Lasso from El Paso, and the Three Amigos.

the World Television Championship. He then moved on to WCW and eventually WWE.

During his WWE Hall of Fame career, Guerrero became known as "Latino Heat." He had a smile that fans loved, but he wanted to win at all costs—even if that meant lying and cheating. He was known for being a tough competitor. He famously used a Frog Splash maneuver to win the WWE Championship in 2004, defeating Brock Lesnar. The victory was notable because Lesnar was larger than Guerrero.

During his career, Guerrero used the phrase "Viva La Raza" in matches. He died of a heart condition in 2005. In tribute after his death, WWE fans shouted "Viva Eddie Guerrero" to remember him.

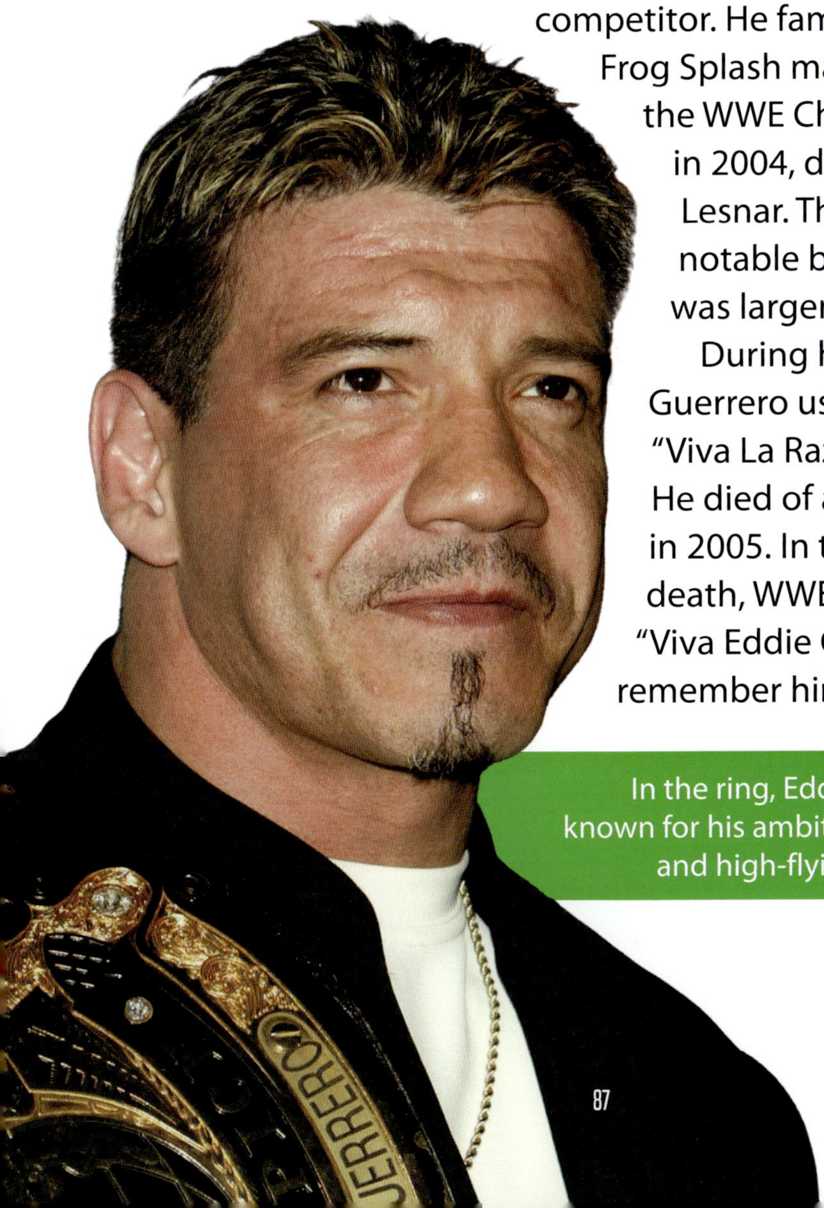

In the ring, Eddie Guerrero was known for his ambitious personality and high-flying aerial moves.

HARDY BOYZ

> **FUN FACT**
>
> The Hardy Boyz teamed up with Lita to form a tag team called Team Xtreme.

The Hardy Boyz are a wrestling duo made up of brothers Matt and Jeff Hardy. The pair revolutionized tag team wrestling, winning multiple WWF Tag Team Championships during the Attitude Era. The high-flying duo defeated teams such as Edge and Christian and the Dudley Boyz. The Hardy Boyz competed in the first Tables, Ladders, and Chairs (TLC) matches too. In these tag team matches, wrestlers use tables, ladders, and chairs as weapons.

The brothers also performed solo in the WWE. Matt won several titles, including the United States, Hardcore, European, and Cruiserweight Championships. In 2002, the Hardy Boyz separated. They reunited at WrestleMania 33 in 2017.

Later, Matt formed a new duo with Bray Wyatt. The two wrestlers were originally rivals, but became partners at WrestleMania 34 when Wyatt helped Matt win the André the Giant Memorial Battle Royal. Jeff Hardy went on to win his first WWE Championship at WWE Armageddon 2008. He continues to compete and was chosen by SmackDown in the 2021 WWE Draft.

Jeff Hardy jumps off the top of a ladder during a battle against his brother at WrestleMania 25. He ended up losing the match.

Matt Hardy, *right*, battles Jeff Hardy, *left*, during WrestleMania 25 in 2009. The brothers had a famous feud throughout the 2000s.

In 2010, Bret Hart appeared at WrestleMania XXVI and defeated Vince McMahon in a memorable match.

BRET "THE HITMAN" HART

Bret "The Hitman" Hart had a Hall of Fame career in the WWE. A renowned competitor, Hart was part of a large family of wrestlers. Hart originally came to WWF as part of the Hart Foundation tag team, competing alongside his brother-in-law, Jim "The Anvil" Neidhart. The pair won the World Tag Team Title twice.

After the duo separated, Hart became a singles competitor. One of the best technical wrestlers in WWE history, Hart was anything but boring in the ring. He wore sunglasses and black and pink tights, and he used an electric guitar as a prop. While Hart was entertaining, he used his techniques to find his opponents' weaknesses and defeat them with his Sharpshooter submission move. Hart won five WWE Championships.

> **FUN FACT**
>
> During the 1990s, Hart pursued various acting roles, including a role in the TV series *Lonesome Dove: The Outlaw Years*.

Hart's career was cut short in 2000, when he was kicked in the head during a PPV match. He suffered a severe concussion. Two years later, he had a stroke and retired from wrestling.

Bret Hart, *bottom*, faces off against his brother Owen Hart during WrestleMania X in 1994.

Jim Neidhart, *left*, and Bret Hart, *center*, pose with their title belts alongside manager Jimmy Hart, *right*, in 1987.

THE HART FOUNDATION

The Hart Foundation was a tag team duo of Bret "The Hitman" Hart and Jim "The Anvil" Neidhart. The brothers-in-law formed a tag team in 1985. They won their first WWF World Tag Team Title in 1987.

Manager Jimmy Hart helped the duo climb the ranks. But when the wrestlers fired him in 1988, Jimmy Hart worked against the duo. He made them the target of other duos he managed, including the Fabulous Rougeaus and the Honky Tonk Man and Greg Valentine.

The Hart Foundation survived Jimmy Hart's attempts to destroy them and focused on winning a World Tag Team Championship. They succeeded at SummerSlam 1990, defeating the tag team Demolition. Hart and Neidhart split up in 1991. They were inducted into the WWE Hall of Fame in 2019.

FUN FACT

Despite their shared last names, Jimmy Hart and Bret Hart are not related.

Jim Neidhart, *second from left*, faces off against Raymond Rougeau, *left*, during a 1987 match at Nassau Coliseum in New York.

Bobby Heenan, *left*, was often involved in wrestling storylines with the stars he managed. In 1990, he appeared in the ring with André the Giant, *right*, at WrestleMania VI.

BOBBY "THE BRAIN" HEENAN

Bobby "The Brain" Heenan was a notorious professional wrestling manager. He was also the genius behind the Heenan Family stable. He managed some of the biggest names in pro wrestling. Heenan helped wrestlers succeed by being a mischievous manager. He made sarcastic comments and acted out on behalf of his wrestlers so he'd get in trouble instead of them. Some of his top

FUN FACT

Some of Heenan's nicknames included the Brain, the Weasel, and Pretty Boy.

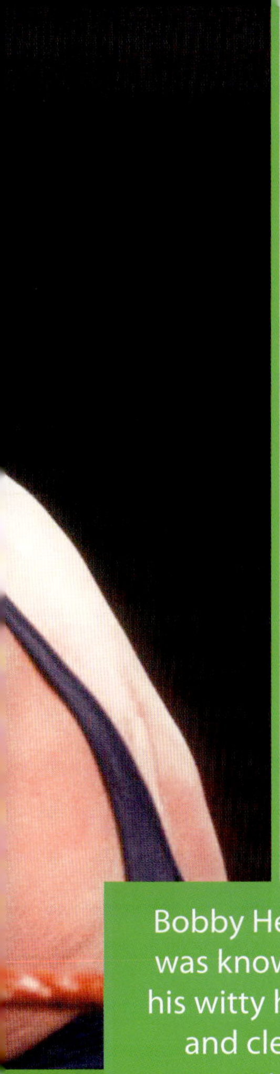

wrestlers included André the Giant, Rick Rude, Curt Hennig, and the Brain Busters.

Heenan also worked as a wrestling announcer. His announcing partner was Gorilla Monsoon. They were known to add humor to their commentary. Heenan was part of the original broadcast team for *Monday Night Raw* in 1993. He was also the only person to announce both Raw and WCW Monday Nitro. Heenan was inducted into the WWE Hall of Fame in 2004. He died in 2017.

Bobby Heenan was known for his witty humor and clever commentary. He also frequently wore sparkly jackets in the ring.

THE HEENAN FAMILY

The Heenan Family was a stable of heels created by manager Bobby Heenan in the 1970s. He called the wrestlers he managed "The Heenan Family" to show that their bond was stronger than a stable. Some of the most famous members of the group included AWA champion Nick Bockwinkel,

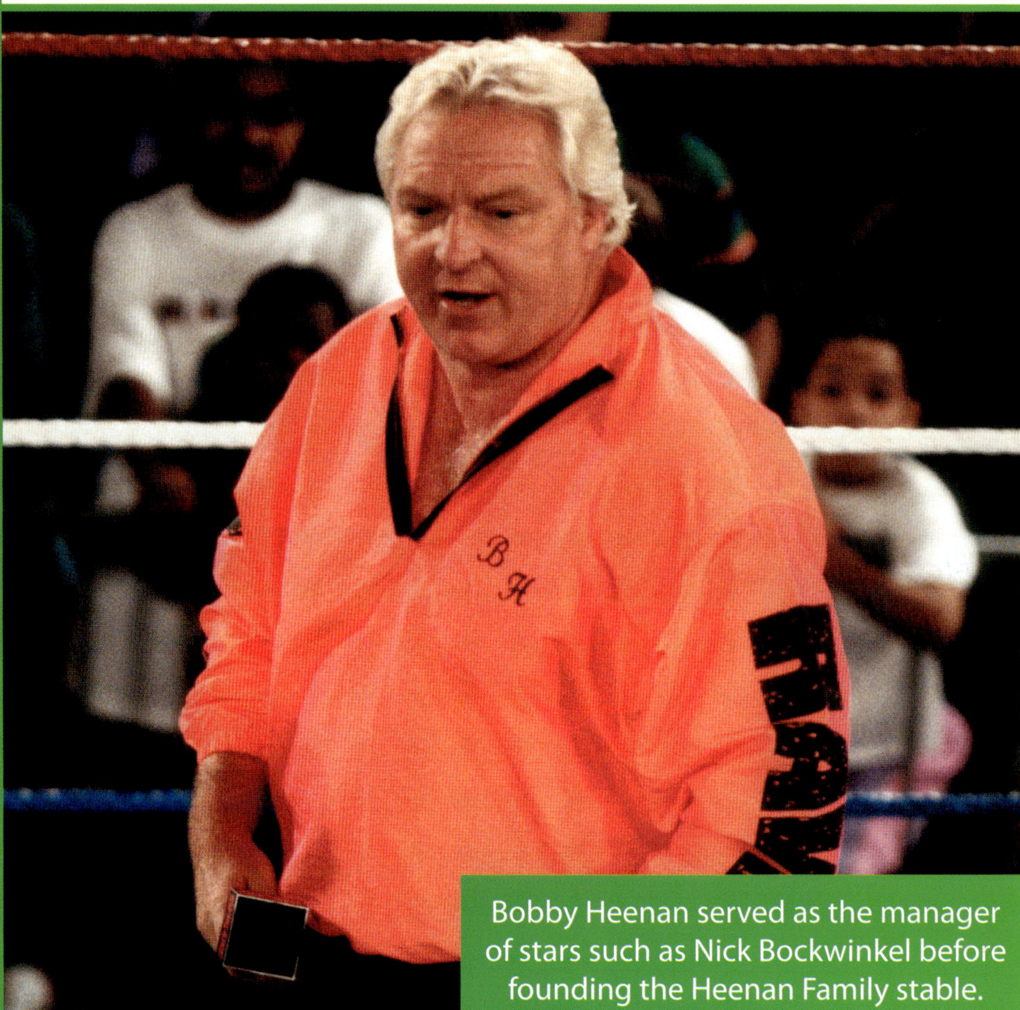

Bobby Heenan served as the manager of stars such as Nick Bockwinkel before founding the Heenan Family stable.

Heenan Family members André the Giant, *left*, and Big John Studd, *right*, feuded throughout the 1980s. Their rivalry became a famous storyline.

the Blackjacks, Big John Studd, King Kong Bundy, and Rick Rude. Other notable members included Curt Hennig, the Brain Busters, Harley Race, and André the Giant.

The Heenan Family didn't find immediate success. It took about four years for the group to earn a title. But once it did, success quickly followed. The group won eight championships during its ten-year run in the WWE.

FUN FACT

Bobby Heenan used the term "family" for The Heenan Family because the term "stable" reminded him of a horse stable.

CURT HENNIG

Curt Hennig was the son of wrestler Larry "The Axe" Hennig. Before joining the WWE, Hennig was part of Verne Gagne's AWA. When he competed in the WWE, Hennig was known as "Mr. Perfect." With his white boots and curly blonde hair, Mr. Perfect was flawless in everything he did. He had perfect wrestling skills and even had a perfect record for about a year after his debut in 1988.

Curt Hennig's first on-screen loss happened at WrestleMania VI in 1990. Hennig, *left*, lost a match against Brutus Beefcake, *right*.

Curt Hennig was known for wearing bright-colored singlets during his matches.

FUN FACT

Curt Hennig was inducted into the WWE Hall of Fame by Major League Baseball (MLB) Hall of Famer Wade Boggs.

Hennig was a two-time world title winner. After suffering several injuries, Hennig became an executive consultant to Ric Flair. In 1996, Hennig led Triple H to an Intercontinental Championship before leaving for WCW. In WCW, Hennig joined the Four Horsemen. But then he switched to the New World Order, a group of villains. In 1999, he joined the West Texas Rednecks. Hennig died in 2003 at the age of 44.

Hulk Hogan, *right*, faces off against The Rock, *bottom*, during an "Icon vs. Icon" match at WrestleMania X8 in 2002. The Rock ended up winning the match.

HULK HOGAN

Hulk Hogan is often considered the most famous pro wrestler. He was known for his large size, charisma, and signature red and yellow costume. He called his muscular biceps "pythons." Hogan's loyal fans called themselves Hulkamaniacs.

A global celebrity, Hogan drew large crowds when he performed. He was the main attraction for many years in both WWF and WCW. A member of the WWE Hall of Fame,

FUN FACT

Hogan chose the name Hulk Hogan because he was bigger than Lou Ferrigno, the actor who played the superhero The Incredible Hulk.

Hogan played many characters throughout his career, including Mr. America. This was a heroic character who wore a red, white, and blue costume. He debuted on SmackDown in 2003.

During his time in WWE, Hogan had many epic battles with other wrestlers. He defeated André the Giant at WrestleMania III in 1987. He also squared off against Randy Savage at WrestleMania V in 1989 and The Rock at WrestleMania X8 in 2002.

In the mid-1990s, Hogan left WWE for WCW. In the new organization, he played a villain and joined the New World Order. Hogan returned to the WWE in 2002.

Hulk Hogan often wore tie-dyed tights and a bandana during his matches. Sometimes he tore his shirt to show that he was ready for a fight.

ANTONIO INOKI

Antonio Inoki was a legendary Japanese wrestler. He was born in 1943 in Yokohama, Japan, but grew up in Brazil. He met Rikidōzan, one of the most famous Japanese wrestlers, and the star convinced him to take up wrestling. In the 1960s, Inoki joined Rikidōzan's Japanese Wrestling Association (JWA) in Tokyo.

FUN FACT

Inoki was beloved in Japan and was elected to the country's House of Councillors in 1989.

In 1976, Antonio Inoki, *left*, and boxer Muhammad Ali, *right*, battled in a 15-round match. It took place in Tokyo, Japan, in front of thousands of fans.

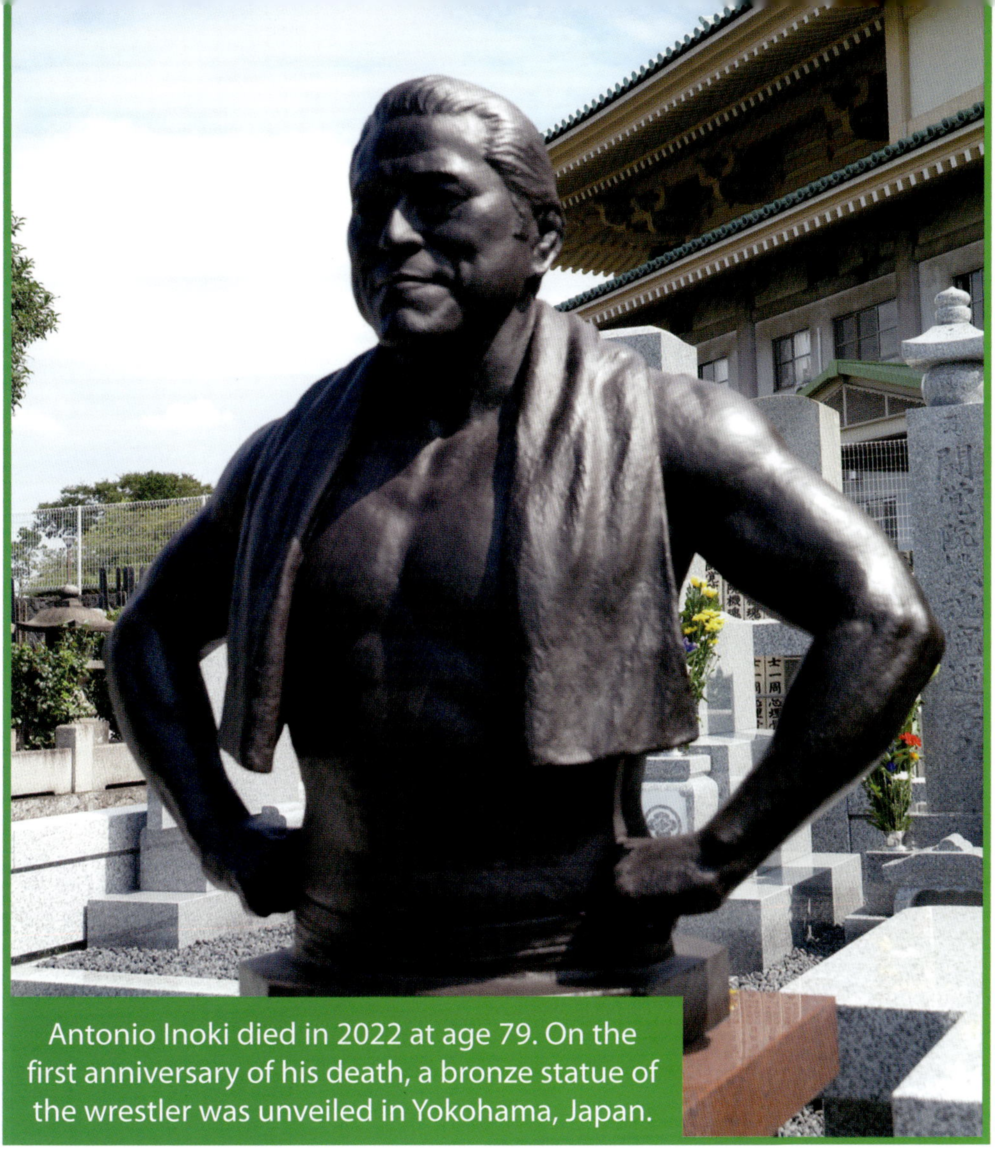

Antonio Inoki died in 2022 at age 79. On the first anniversary of his death, a bronze statue of the wrestler was unveiled in Yokohama, Japan.

In the JWA, Inoki found success in tag team wrestling. But his biggest successes came after 1972, when he founded New Japan Pro Wrestling (NJPW). It became Asia's most successful wrestling company, featuring the top Japanese wrestlers and even some American stars.

Inoki also competed for NJPW. His biggest fight happened in Tokyo on June 26, 1976. He squared off against celebrity Muhammad Ali in a wrestler versus boxer fight.

CHRIS JERICHO

Chris Jericho is known for his rock star–inspired wrestling persona. Outside of wrestling, he is also part of a heavy-metal band called Fozzy.

Chris Jericho was a confident pro wrestler who wasn't afraid to take bold actions in his matches. This made him a fan favorite and a fierce competitor in the ring. After training at the Hart Brothers School of Wrestling, Jericho made his pro-wrestling debut in 1990 at age 19. He competed in Canada, Mexico, and Japan. He then went to the ECW and the WCW. He won several WCW championships, growing a fan base of "Jerichoholics."

Jericho moved to WWE in 1999. For his debut, a clock counted down the moments until his arrival. Nicknamed "the Ayatollah of Rock 'n' Rolla," Jericho won nine Intercontinental titles, along with seven WWE and World Tag Team titles. In 2001, he became the WWE's first undisputed champion when he defeated The Rock to win the WCW World Heavyweight Title and defeated "Stone Cold" Steve Austin for the WWE Championship.

FUN FACT

Chris Jericho is the son of former National Hockey League (NHL) player Ted Irvine.

Chris Jericho appears in the ring at the 2023 AEW All In event in London, England.

KANE

Kane was said to be Undertaker's half brother. Undertaker supposedly burned Kane in a fire when they were kids. Kane wore a mask and sought revenge. Their rivalry captivated WWE fans in the late 1990s and into the 2000s.

Standing nearly seven feet (2.1 m) tall, Kane was nicknamed "The Big Red Monster." He became known for his destructive ways, such as setting an opponent on fire. Kane and Undertaker faced off in many memorable matches. They also joined forces as a tag team called the Brothers of Destruction.

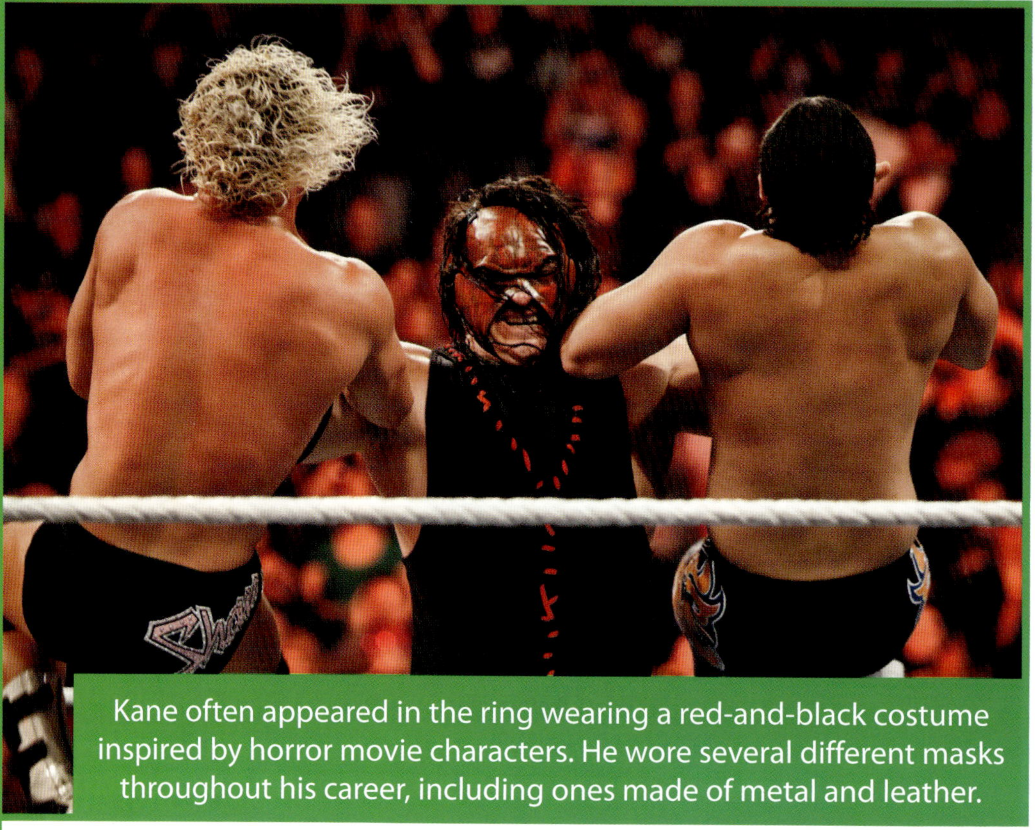

Kane often appeared in the ring wearing a red-and-black costume inspired by horror movie characters. He wore several different masks throughout his career, including ones made of metal and leather.

Kane, *center*, battles Chavo Guerrero Jr., *left*, during a 2008 match in Sydney, Australia.

FUN FACT

Glenn Jacobs, who played Kane, was later elected mayor of Knox County, Tennessee.

Kane's character evolved greatly over the years. Later in his career, he took his mask off. Kane found great success in the ring. He held the WWE and World Heavyweight championships.

In 2011, Jerry Lawler attended the WWE *Monday Night Raw SuperShow* Halloween event. He served as a commentator.

JERRY LAWLER

Jerry "The King" Lawler starred as a pro wrestler inside the ring before becoming a Raw announcer outside of the ring. A WWE Hall of Famer, Lawler gained fans during a feud with comedian Andy Kaufman. Their rivalry went back and forth. During a 1982 interview on the TV show *Late Night with David Letterman*, Lawler even slapped Kaufman.

Lawler made his WWE debut in 1992 as a wrestler. He never won a WWE championship, but he competed in many memorable fights. He almost defeated The Miz at Elimination Chamber in 2011.

That same year, he competed against fellow announcer Michael Cole at WrestleMania XXVII. Lawler has also appeared on WWE as a commentator. He and partner Jim Ross called fights during the Attitude Era.

Jerry Lawler often appeared in the ring dressed as a king. His costumes featured royal robes, tights, and a crown.

FUN FACT

Jerry Lawler's cousin is wrestler Roy Wayne Farris, better known as the Honky Tonk Man.

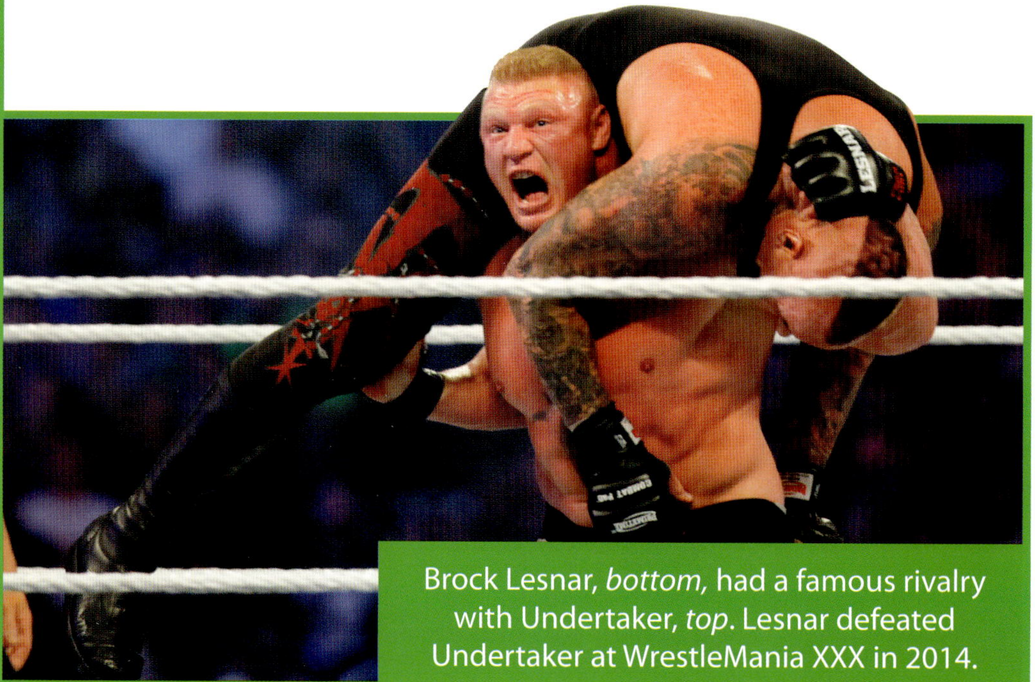

Brock Lesnar, *bottom,* had a famous rivalry with Undertaker, *top*. Lesnar defeated Undertaker at WrestleMania XXX in 2014.

BROCK LESNAR

With his large physique and incredible strength, Brock Lesnar dominated the WWE. A champion collegiate wrestler, Lesnar debuted on Raw in 2002. He competed as The Next Big Thing, a heel. Lesnar dominated his competition from the start. He won the 2002 King of the Ring tournament. He also beat The Rock to become the youngest WWE Champion at age 25.

For most of his WWE career, Lesnar wrestled as The Beast Incarnate. He dominated from 2012 to 2020. His fans started the chant "Suplex City" after Lesnar hit John Cena with 13 German suplexes, or throws, in a 2014 match. Lesnar won multiple WWE Championships. He also

FUN FACT

Lesnar played in preseason football games with the Minnesota Vikings in 2004.

became the first wrestler to defeat Undertaker at WrestleMania in 2014.

In 2021, Lesnar began wrestling as The Babyface. During matches, he sported a beard, ponytail, and overalls. Outside of wrestling, Lesnar was also a star in the Ultimate Fighting Championship (UFC), a mixed martial arts organization. In 2024, he was still appearing in some wrestling events.

Brock Lesnar faces off against Randy Orton, *bottom*, during WWE SummerSlam in 2016. Lesnar went on to win the match.

LITA

A four-time Women's Champion, Lita was an acrobatic WWE wrestler known for her high-flying moves in the ring. She made her WWE debut in 2000 alongside Essa Rios. After helping Rios win a Light Heavyweight Championship, Lita teamed up with the Hardy Boyz to form Team Xtreme.

FUN FACT

Lita has the word "PUNK" tattooed on the inside of her lip.

Lita, *center*, worked with the Hardy Boyz as part of Team Xtreme for almost five years.

Lita won her first Women's Championship in 2000. She defeated Stephanie McMahon. McMahon, Vince McMahon's daughter, was a WWE owner and wrestler.

Lita's biggest rival was Trish Stratus. The two wrestlers had epic showdowns featuring Lita's agile moves and Stratus's techniques. Their rivalry helped them gain fans, and their matches became must-see events. In a 2004 Survivor Series match, Lita was disqualified for hitting Stratus with a chair.

Throughout her wrestling career, Lita was involved in storylines with Matt Hardy, Kane, and Edge. She announced her retirement from professional wrestling in 2006. In 2014, she was inducted into the WWE Hall of Fame.

In 2019, Lita attended SmackDown's 20th Anniversary Celebration in Los Angeles, California.

LEX LUGER

Former bodybuilder Lex Luger was originally known as The Narcissist. This character was an arrogant heel who was obsessed with himself and his muscular build. Luger's personality and confidence helped him find success in the ring.

Luger debuted in WCW in 1987, partnering with the Four Horsemen. He was one of the first non-original members to join the group. Six months after joining WCW, Luger defeated Nikita Koloff to win his first United States Championship. He eventually left the Four Horsemen to develop an independent wrestling identity. In 1988, he challenged Ric Flair for the WCW/NWA Heavyweight Championship.

Lex Luger, *left*, faces off against the wrestler Crush, *right*, in 1999.

In July 1993, Luger began wrestling as The All-American, a character focused on American pride. On July 4 of that year, he competed against WWE champion Yokozuna on the deck of the ship USS *Intrepid*. As The All-American, Luger traveled the country in a red, white, and blue Lex Express bus.

In 1995, Luger returned to WCW as The Total Package. He defeated Hulk Hogan to win his second WCW Championship. He became the first WCW competitor to beat the nWo leader for the title. In 1998, Luger joined The nWo Wolfpac.

FUN FACT

Vince McMahon gave Lex Luger the nickname "The All-American."

Lex Luger's real name is Lawrence "Larry" Wendell Pfohl. As a wrestler, he became well-known for his impressive physique.

BECKY LYNCH

Determined to reach the top of the ranks, Irish wrestler Becky Lynch has overcome disappointment and defeat to win. She has taken on many different wrestling personas throughout her career. Nicknamed The Man, she is known for fighting anyone who gets in her way.

In 2018, Lynch and Ronda Rousey faced off in the SmackDown Women's Championship. Despite getting a concussion, Lynch won, claiming her second title. Lynch also won the 2019 Royal Rumble Match, earning a chance to win a World Championship at WrestleMania 35. This was the first women's main event in WrestleMania history. Lynch defeated Rousey and Charlotte Flair.

Becky Lynch holds up her title belt during *Monday Night Raw* in May 2019.

Becky Lynch leaps from the ropes during a match against Rhea Ripley, *bottom*, at WrestleMania 40 in 2024. Lynch's costume for the match featured pages from a book she wrote.

FUN FACT

Lynch has had numerous jobs outside of wrestling. She has worked as a personal trainer, Hollywood stuntwoman, and flight attendant. She also taught English as a second language.

Lynch was the longest-reigning Raw Women's Champion. Her streak ended in 2020, when she announced her pregnancy and gave up her title. But Lynch later returned to pro wrestling. In 2023, she became a Triple Crown Champion after winning her third title at the WWE Women's Tag Team Championship. Later that year, Lynch was crowned a Grand Slam Champion.

In 2024, Stephanie McMahon appeared in the ring to kick off the second night of WrestleMania 40.

STEPHANIE McMAHON

Stephanie McMahon, the daughter of Vince McMahon, has been involved in WWE as both a wrestler and executive. She worked behind the scenes, in the front office, and in the ring to keep WWE running. Until resigning in 2023, McMahon served as the organization's principal owner, co-CEO, and chief brand officer.

FUN FACT

McMahon has never teamed up with a female wrestler in a match. She has always had male tag team partners.

When she was a teen, McMahon modeled T-shirts in the WWE catalog. Later, she became SmackDown's general manager, wrestled as part of the Authority stable, and served as the Raw commissioner. McMahon was also part of a rivalry between WWE and the Ministry of Darkness stable.

As a wrestler, McMahon played herself. One of her biggest storylines involved her real-life husband, Triple H, who was her father's rival. McMahon and Triple H were also fictionally married in WWE. They teamed up in the ring, taking on Ronda Rousey and Kurt Angle at WrestleMania in 2018.

McMahon has competed solo in the ring, too, earning a Women's Champion title. Outside of wrestling, McMahon supports the Be a STAR anti-bullying campaign. She also helps with charity projects.

At WrestleMania X8 in 2002, Stephanie McMahon, *left*, appeared in the ring with Triple H, *right*. The real-life couple were pitted against each other in the match.

VINCE McMAHON

Vince McMahon turned professional wrestling into a profitable and popular sports-entertainment enterprise. McMahon bought WWE, then called WWF, from his father in 1982. He turned the organization into a major entertainment institution. He brought music, celebrities, and flashy costumes into the scripted matches.

McMahon created must-see events that attracted hundreds of thousands of fans. These events drew large in-person crowds and PPV audiences. McMahon also created nationally-televised programs such as *Raw* and *SmackDown*, which helped WWE

In 2009, Vince McMahon, *second from left*, appeared in a *Monday Night Raw* match with Triple H, John Cena, and Shawn Michaels.

attract a nationwide fan base. While WWE became popular in the 1990s for its over-the-top entertainment, McMahon toned down the storylines by 2009. He made the violence more unrealistic to ensure audiences knew it was fake.

McMahon also starred in storylines and worked as an announcer. He had memorable showdowns with his daughter, Stephanie, including one in which she was forced to resign as general manager of SmackDown after McMahon defeated her. McMahon also gave himself the WWE Championship when "Stone Cold" Steve Austin helped him defeat Triple H.

In 2022, McMahon stepped down as WWE chairman and CEO after facing legal actions and accusations. He returned as executive chairman in 2023. But McMahon was forced out in 2024.

In the ring, Vince McMahon often took on the persona of a villainous boss. He was part of many major WWE storylines.

FUN FACT

In 2000, McMahon created the XFL in an attempt to compete with the NFL.

Shawn Michaels, *top*, battles Randy Orton during a WWE Cyber Sunday match in 2007. Michaels ended up defeating Orton.

SHAWN MICHAELS

Throughout his Hall of Fame career, Shawn Michaels won every major WWE title and two Royal Rumbles. Called The Heartbreak Kid, or HBK, he was a notorious rebel in the ring. In his storylines, he constantly made life hard for the McMahon family and partnered with Triple H to cause trouble. Michaels was also a founding member of D-Generation X and a member of the Kliq stable.

Michaels was known for intimidating competitors into giving him and his allies preferential treatment. He was also involved in a notorious match against Bret "The Hitman" Hart at the 1997 Survivor Series. Michaels defeated Hart to win

FUN FACT

Shawn Michaels was the fourth Triple Crown winner in WWE history, meaning he has won three of the promotion's championships.

the title. Michaels locked Hart in a hold. Before Hart could free himself, the referee ended the match.

Michaels's career was almost cut short when he suffered a back injury in a 1998 match against Undertaker. The injury kept him from wrestling for more than four years. In 2002 Michaels returned to action, eventually competing in his final match at WrestleMania XXVI in 2010.

Shawn Michaels walks past fans on his way to a public workout event for WrestleMania XIV in 1998.

JON MOXLEY (DEAN AMBROSE)

A vicious and intense competitor, Dean Ambrose had a message for his WWE opponents: "No one is safe." After competing for independent organizations, Ambrose made his WWE debut in 2012. Known as "The Lunatic Fringe," he wasn't

Dean Ambrose is a fan-favorite wrestler known for being energetic and unpredictable in the ring. He is often involved in intense matches.

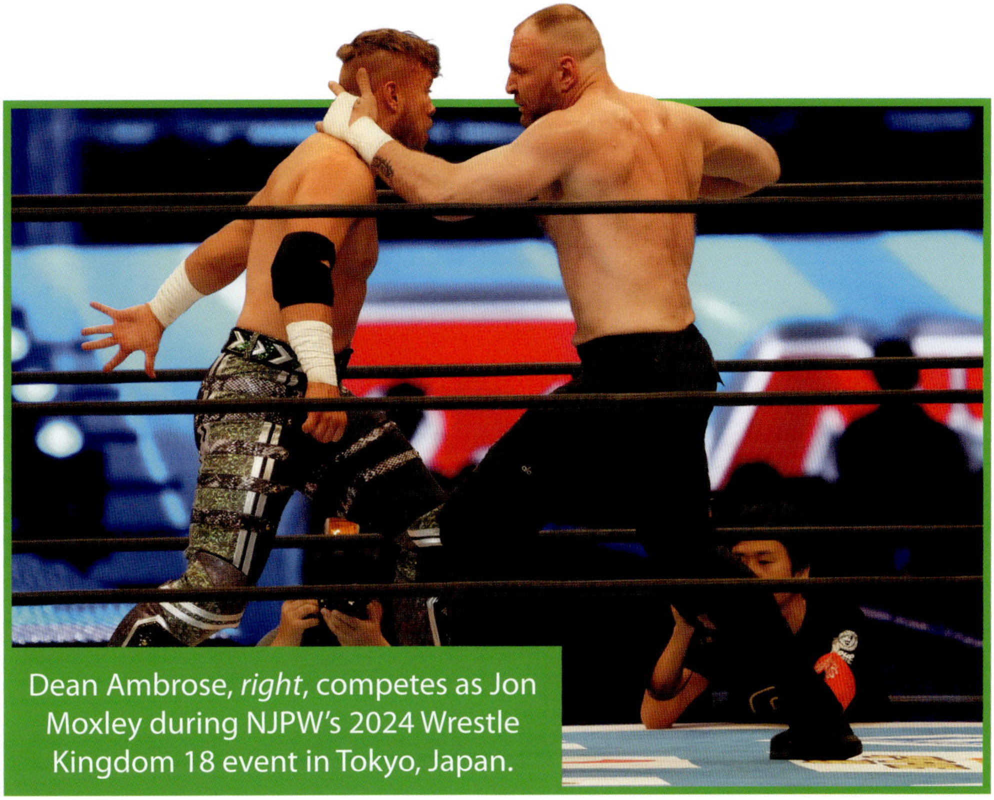

Dean Ambrose, *right*, competes as Jon Moxley during NJPW's 2024 Wrestle Kingdom 18 event in Tokyo, Japan.

afraid to shed blood or hurt his opponents in matches. This attitude helped him become a US Champion in May 2013. He held the title for a record 351 days.

In June 2016, Ambrose won his first WWE world championship title at Money in the Bank. He also won two WWE Raw Tag Team Championships with Seth Rollins and is a WWE Grand Slam winner. Ambrose was a member of the Shield stable with Roman Reigns and Rollins. On April 21, 2019, the Shield competed in their final match together. That same year, Ambrose joined AEW as Jon Moxley. He continued to appear in events throughout 2024.

FUN FACT

Ambrose starred in the 2015 film *12 Rounds 3: Lockdown*.

Rey Mysterio, *top*, is sometimes called "The Biggest Little Man." His real name is Oscar Gutierrez.

REY MYSTERIO JR.

Mexican wrestler Rey Mysterio has a unique style inspired by *lucha libre* wrestling. He became famous for wearing a mask in his matches and entertaining fans with his energetic moves. He helped introduce *lucha libre* to fans in the United States.

Known as "The Ultimate Underdog," Mysterio first performed in ECW and WCW. Mysterio and his rival, Psicosis, helped elevate ECW in the mid-1990s. After some of the organization's top stars left, Mysterio and Psicosis used their unique style to gain fans.

Mysterio joined the WWE in 2002. At WrestleMania 22 in 2006, he became the smallest star to win the World

Heavyweight Championship at five feet, six inches (1.7 m) tall. One of Mysterio's most famous WWE matches was against Chris Jericho in The Bash in 2009. This was a cruiserweight-style match, meaning it was fast-paced and featured many jumps. Jericho tried to remove Mysterio's mask during the match. But Mysterio defeated Jericho and won the Intercontinental Championship. Mysterio was inducted into the WWE Hall of Fame in 2023. In 2024, he was still competing.

FUN FACT

Mysterio's son, Dominik, is also a professional wrestler. His major career appearances began in 2019.

Rey Mysterio, *masked*, grapples with opponent Chris Jericho during the WCW Bash at the Beach event in 1998.

KEVIN NASH

For part of his career, Kevin Nash was nicknamed "Diesel" and wore biker-style costumes in the ring.

Kevin Nash was a formidable foe, standing nearly seven feet (2.1 m) tall. But his success wasn't immediate. After joining WCW in 1990, Nash struggled to find his identity. His career got a boost in 1993 when he joined WWE. He started as Shawn Michaels's bodyguard, meaning his role was to protect Michaels and ensure he won matches.

In 1996, Nash and Scott Hall went back to WCW, beginning a major storyline that involved them "invading" WCW and forming the New World Order (nWo) stable. Nash and Hall found success as a duo, but when Hulk Hogan joined nWo, it transformed the world of pro wrestling. The wrestler Syxx also joined the nWo. The stable quickly became the WCW's most popular storyline.

Kevin Nash, *left*, speaks at the 2019 German Comic Con in Dortmund, Germany.

FUN FACT

Kevin Nash has appeared in numerous movies, including the 2005 film *The Longest Yard*.

Nash eventually formed his own group, the Wolfpac. Later, he moved to WWE when WCW shut down in 2001. He retired from wrestling in 2020.

NATION OF DOMINATION

The Nation of Domination was a WWE stable active during the Attitude Era. With storylines loosely based on real-life civil rights issues, the diverse group of heels helped put Black wrestlers on the big stage. Many wrestlers joined Nation of Domination, including some of WWE's most successful stars. Ron Simmons, D'Lo Brown, the Godfather, The Rock, and Mark Henry were all members. The Nation of Domination not only played a big role in adding diverse storylines to WWE but also helped launch The Rock's career.

When The Rock joined the Nation of Domination in 1997, it marked the first time he turned into a heel. His involvement with the stable led to later successes, including a victory at WrestleMania XXVIII in 2012.

The Nation of Domination was officially introduced at Royal Rumble 1997. Originally, Faarooq led the group. In March 1998, The Rock took over as the leader, and the group changed its name to The Nation. Its members took on more relaxed characters,

FUN FACT

D'Lo Brown was the longest-running member of The Nation of Domination.

such as The Rock's cool-guy image. While the group worked to help The Rock dominate, it also had a rivalry with D-Generation X. The stable disbanded in October 1998.

In 2011, former Nation of Domination member Mark Henry attended a charity event in Los Angeles, California.

THE NEW WORLD ORDER (nWo)

The New World Order (nWo) was a game-changing stable in WCW. It was an aggressive group of wrestlers on a mission to take control of WCW, like a street gang. It quickly became a fan-favorite stable, dominating the world of pro wrestling.

Scott Hall and Kevin Nash started the stable in 1996. But the group soared in popularity when fan favorite Hulk Hogan joined its roster. He stopped wearing his signature yellow and red costume and started wearing the nWo's rebellious black and white colors. This marked a major change in Hogan's character.

Hulk Hogan famously became the third member of nWo during WCW's Bash at the Beach event in 1996. Many fans were surprised to see Hogan turn heel and join the group.

Founding nWo member Scott Hall, *left*, competes at WrestleMania X8 in 2002. He originally wrestled under the name Razor Ramon.

The stable's members faced off against many major stars from the Attitude Era. The nWo transitioned to WWE after WCW shut down in 2001. The stable was inducted into the WWE Hall of Fame in 2020.

FUN FACT

More than 60 people have been associated with nWo.

"Mean" Gene Okerlund, *right*, worked as a commentator and interviewer for AWA, WWE, and WCW. Wrestler Jesse Ventura gave Okerlund his nickname.

"MEAN" GENE OKERLUND

"Mean" Gene Okerlund was a longtime pro-wrestling announcer, interviewer, and commentator. He started his career in the 1970s as a backstage AWA interviewer. Okerlund moved to WWE in 1984. He worked as a locker room interviewer and did ringside commentary. In 1985, Okerlund sang the national anthem at the first WrestleMania.

Okerlund was linked to Hulk Hogan throughout his career. In their backstage interviews, Hogan would commonly start by saying, "Let me tell you something, 'Mean' Gene." Okerlund helped boost Hogan's popularity by showcasing his personality to audiences. He gave Hogan the opportunity to speak to his fans. Okerlund was inducted into the WWE Hall of Fame in 2006. He died in 2019.

FUN FACT

Early in his career, Okerlund worked as a disc jockey at a radio station in Omaha, Nebraska.

"Mean" Gene Okerlund, *second from left*, appeared in the ring during *Monday Night Raw* in 2010.

KENNY OMEGA

Canadian wrestler Kenny Omega is known for his stints in smaller wrestling organizations, as well for his role as the executive vice president of All Elite Wrestling (AEW). In the ring, Omega often incorporates elements from video games into his personas. Nicknamed "the Cleaner," Omega wears costumes and uses wrestling moves inspired by video game characters. He also uses video game themes as his entrance music. The villain Sephiroth from the game *Final Fantasy 7* inspired Omega's character.

Omega started his pro-wrestling career in Premier Championship Wrestling (PCW) in the early 2000s. In the mid-2000s, Omega started competing in NJPW. He competed individually and as part of a tag team. He became a heel in 2014, joining the

Kenny Omega has several nicknames, including the Best Bout Machine. His real name is Tyson Smith.

Kenny Omega, *center*, competes during the AEW All In event in London, England.

FUN FACT

Kenny Omega is fluent in Japanese.

Bullet Club stable. He later became the group's leader. In 2019, Omega joined AEW. In 2024, he was still competing in matches.

RANDY ORTON

Randy Orton stands on the ropes during WrestleMania XXX in 2014. He competed in the main event.

Randy Orton was born into a professional wrestling family. His grandfather and uncle wrestled, and his dad is WWE Hall of Famer "Cowboy" Bob Orton. Orton followed them into the family business. Eventually, he became the biggest star of them all.

Orton won his first World Heavyweight Championship in 2004, just two years after debuting in WWE. He has won multiple Royal Rumble Matches and WWE World Heavyweight titles. Orton has also portrayed numerous characters, including The Legend Killer. His mission was to take down every WWE legend he encountered, including The Fabulous Moolah and Jerry "The King" Lawler. This character was the foundation for Orton's other character, The Apex Predator or The Viper. This persona is snakelike and sneaky.

Orton suffered a back injury in May 2022, and many people thought

FUN FACT

Orton started his career as a wrestling referee.

the injury would end his career. However, Orton returned to wrestling a year and a half later at Survivor Series: WarGames. He later signed on to be a SmackDown Superstar.

Randy Orton, *right*, had feuds and rivalries with many wrestlers, including Umaga, *left*.

"DIAMOND" DALLAS PAGE

WWE Hall of Famer "Diamond" Dallas Page was a wrestler and manager. Often called DDP, Page started his career in 1988 as an AWA manager. He created the Diamond Mine stable. In 1991, he left to manage in WCW. Later that year, he started wrestling. He went on to win numerous titles, including three WCW World Heavyweight titles and four WCW World Tag Team Championships.

In the mid-1990s, Page wrestled as a heel and was involved in storylines with his wife, The Diamond Doll, and bodyguard, Max Muscle. He became a babyface in 1997 and had a famous feud with nWo. During this time, Page transformed into a main event star. He commonly used a diamond hand gesture and maneuver during matches. Both were known as The Diamond Cutter.

"Diamond" Dallas Page often used his Diamond Cutter hand gesture to create excitement before matches, taunt his opponents, or celebrate a victory.

"Diamond" Dallas Page, *top*, reacts during a match against Christian, *bottom right*, at WrestleMania X8 in 2002.

When WCW ended in 2001, Page joined WWE. He debuted on Raw in the main event of the PPV event Invasion. After suffering numerous injuries, Page left WWE in 2002.

FUN FACT

Page created a yoga program called DDP Yoga after using the exercise to help recover from a back injury.

In 2005, "Rowdy" Roddy Piper appeared at WrestleMania 21 wearing his trademark Scottish kilt.

"ROWDY" RODDY PIPER

"Rowdy" Roddy Piper was one of the biggest villains in WWE history. He joined the organization in 1984 after spending years in the NWA. Piper, who wore a Scottish kilt and used bagpipes as his entrance music, used dirty antics to defeat his rivals.

FUN FACT

Piper was also an actor. He had a starring role in the 1988 film *They Live*.

He was known for his short temper and memorable feuds, including one with singer Cyndi Lauper.

Piper's heated exchanges with competitors helped the WWE's popularity soar. He also attracted fans by creating controversies, such as breaking one of Lauper's gold records. In the 1980s, he competed on the cable channel MTV and headlined the first WrestleMania.

From 1984 to 1987, Piper hosted "Piper's Pit," a TV segment in which he interviewed wrestlers. He was often mean to guests and tried to upset them. Piper won his first championship in 1992, defeating The Mountie to win the Intercontinental Championship. In 2006, he won the World Tag Team Title with Ric Flair. Piper was inducted into the WWE Hall of Fame in 2005.

"Rowdy" Roddy Piper, *right*, battles Chris Jericho, *center*, during WrestleMania 25 in 2009. Piper teamed up with Ricky Steamboat and Jimmy Snuka to take on Jericho.

CM PUNK

CM Punk is a rebellious, confrontational, and outspoken WWE wrestler. He flaunts tattoos and body piercings. He has played both a hero and villain, altering his personality to fit different roles.

Punk competed on smaller wrestling circuits before joining WWE in 2006. As a heel, Punk was known for feuding with Jeff Hardy and Edge. He dressed up as Hardy and mocked Hardy's drug and alcohol issues. Punk eventually defeated Hardy in a steel cage match, gaining popularity as a villain. He showed another personality when he formed the Straight Edge Society stable. He encouraged members to adopt a "straight edge"

CM Punk, *top*, leaps off the ropes during a match against Randy Orton at WrestleMania XXVII in 2011. The two wrestlers had a rivalry.

CM Punk, *standing*, lifts opponent Chris Jericho during WrestleMania XXVIII. He ended up defeating Jericho.

lifestyle, or one against using drugs and alcohol. He made members shave their heads to show their devotion.

CM Punk won the ECW, WWE, World Heavyweight, World Tag Team, and Intercontinental championships. However, he had real-life issues with WWE. Punk left WWE in 2014 because he felt like he wasn't respected and didn't get enough headline matches at WrestleMania. He later joined AEW in 2021. Punk made a highly anticipated return to WWE in 2023 to try to recapture his past success.

FUN FACT

The "CM" in CM Punk's name stands for "Chick Magnet."

Harley Race was the second person to win the King of the Ring tournament. The victory inspired his king gimmick.

HARLEY RACE

With a career spanning five decades, Harley Race won many titles as a pro wrestler. He won three AWA World Tag Team Championships, eight NWA World Heavyweight Championships, and the NWA World Team Championship. Race dominated wrestling throughout the 1970s and 1980s. He even nicknamed himself the Greatest Wrestler on God's Green Earth.

FUN FACT

Harley Race was managed by his real-life friend Bobby Heenan.

In 1986, Race joined WWE. He won the King of the Ring tournament in 1986 and began calling himself "The King" Harley Race. At WrestleMania III, he competed wearing royal robes and a crown. Race became a heel and had feuds with wrestlers who portrayed the common man. One match featured Race competing against Junkyard Dog at WrestleMania III in 1987. Race won, making Junkyard Dog bow down to him. But then Junkyard Dog stole Race's cape.

Race is one of only six men to have been inducted into the WWE Hall of Fame, NWA Hall of Fame, WCW Hall of Fame, Professional Wrestling Hall of Fame, and Wrestling Observer Newsletter Hall of Fame. He died in 2019.

Harley Race, *center*, had rivalries with many notable wrestlers, including Dusty Rhodes, *left*.

ROMAN REIGNS

Roman Reigns never shied away from a challenge, whether it was inside or outside the ring. He made his WWE debut in the mid-2010s. Known for his tattoos and long dark hair, Reigns was the enforcer in the popular Shield stable. Made up of Reigns, Seth Rollins, and Dean Ambrose, the Shield took out bad guys and called themselves the Hounds of Justice. Later, the group became heels.

In 2018, Reigns defeated his biggest rival, The Beast Incarnate, to win the Universal Championship at SummerSlam. However, Reigns had to give up his title due to a real-life health condition. Leati Joseph Anoa'i, who plays Reigns, announced

Roman Reigns, *left*, holds up his title belt at the 2022 WWE Clash at the Castle. He retained his WWE Universal Championship title at the event.

Roman Reigns leaps over Seth Rollins during WrestleMania 40 in 2024. The former partners have had a long rivalry and are frequently involved in storylines together.

that his leukemia had returned. He was diagnosed with the disease in 2007 and had been in remission until that point. He later recovered and returned as Reigns at SummerSlam 2020.

Reigns created the Bloodline stable in 2021. The group included many members of the Anoa'i family, including Reigns, his cousins The Usos, Solo Sikoa, and Sami Zayn. The Bloodline dominated the WWE, becoming a popular storyline. Reigns became the longest-reigning universal champion and won the 2022 WWE Championship.

FUN FACT

Roman Reigns played football at Georgia Tech before his pro-wrestling career.

CODY RHODES

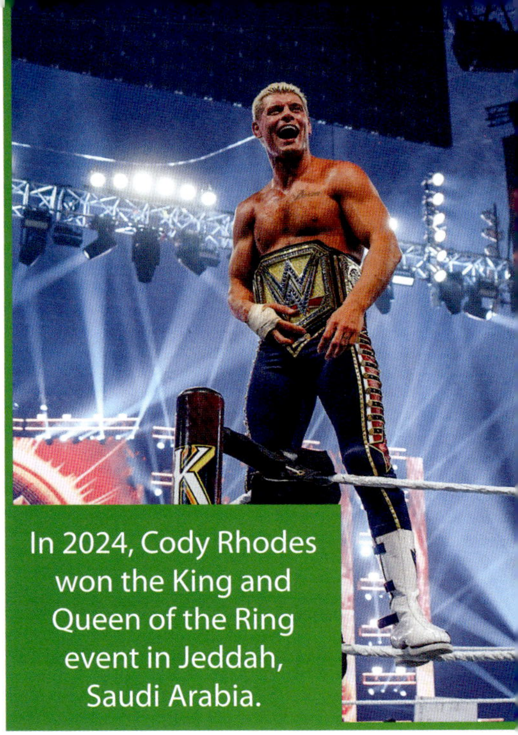

In 2024, Cody Rhodes won the King and Queen of the Ring event in Jeddah, Saudi Arabia.

As the son of WWE Hall of Famer Dusty Rhodes, Cody Rhodes began wrestling at a young age. In 2007, he made his WWE debut on the Raw roster. He quickly achieved success, earning the nickname The American Nightmare in contrast to his father's nickname, The American Dream. In the ring, he took on the persona of "Dashing" Cody Rhodes, a charismatic, self-obsessed babyface. Rhodes won two WWE Intercontinental Championships and six Tag Team Championships.

In 2016, Rhodes left WWE. He was involved in creating AEW in 2019, signing on as the organization's co-executive vice president. Rhodes also competed in AEW matches, winning the first-ever TNT Championship in 2020.

Two years later, Rhodes returned to WWE at WrestleMania 38, defeating Seth Rollins. Rhodes became involved in storylines with the Bloodline and frequently faced off against wrestlers such as Roman Reigns. In 2024, Rhodes fought his way to the top to claim the Royal Rumble title. Later that year, he defeated Reigns at WrestleMania XL to claim the Undisputed WWE Universal Title.

FUN FACT

In the mid-2010s, Rhodes wrestled under the name Stardust. He competed alongside his half brother, Goldust.

Cody Rhodes battles Roman Reigns during WrestleMania XL in 2024. The event took place in Philadelphia, Pennsylvania.

RHEA RIPLEY

Rhea Ripley's strength and aggressive wrestling style make her an intimidating foe. Nicknamed The Nightmare, the Australian powerhouse is known for her tough personality.

Rhea Ripley celebrates after winning a 2023 Royal Rumble Match in San Antonio, Texas.

She frequently wears gothic, heavy metal–inspired costumes.

Ripley made her WWE debut in 2017, competing on the NXT roster. The next year, she became the first-ever WWE UK NXT Women's Champion. Ripley went on to successfully challenge Charlotte Flair for the NXT Women's Championship title at WrestleMania 36 in 2020. She also beat Asuka to claim the 2021 Raw Women's Championship.

In 2022, Ripley joined The Judgement Day, a stable of heels. A year later, Ripley claimed the 2023 Women's Royal Rumble title. She went on to win her first SmackDown Women's Championship at WrestleMania 39. Ripley held the Women's World Champion title for a year until giving it up in 2024 due to injuries.

FUN FACT

Since 2022, Rhea Ripley has used the song "Demon in Your Dreams" as her entrance music.

Rhea Ripley holds the record for the longest Women's World Champion title reign. She held the title for 380 days.

THE ROAD WARRIORS

The Road Warriors are considered one of the best tag teams in the history of pro wrestling. The team included wrestlers Hawk and Animal, along with their manager Precious Paul Ellering. The pair had an intimidating look with mohawk hairstyles, motorcycle boots, and spiky leather. They quickly achieved success, winning the NWA National Tag Team Title in 1983. The Road Warriors dominated the wrestling world over the next two decades.

Hawk, *left*, and Animal, *right*, often wore face paint as part of their wrestling costumes. The duo was known for their frightening appearance during matches.

Animal's real name was Joseph Laurinaitis. He made his pro-wrestling debut alongside Hawk in 1983.

The Road Warriors changed their name to the Legion of Doom when they joined WWE in 1990. The next year, they won the World Tag Team Championship at SummerSlam. They were the only duo to hold the tag team titles in the AWA, NWA, and WWE. Hawk died in 2003, ending the legendary duo's run. Animal died in 2020.

FUN FACT

In one brief storyline, a doll named Rocco was used to motivate the Road Warriors during matches.

During matches, Jake "The Snake" Roberts, *left*, often brought one of his pet snakes into the ring in a bag. He'd use the snake to intimidate his opponents.

JAKE "THE SNAKE" ROBERTS

Jake "The Snake" Roberts became known for using pythons as part of his wrestling antics. But his snakes were only part of his appeal. The son of famous wrestler Grizzly Smith, Roberts started competing in the 1970s. He won the NWA World Television Championship in 1983 before moving to WWE in 1986.

Roberts, who had a signature DDT finishing move, also hosted a weekly talk show called "The Snake Pit." It gave him the opportunity to make enemies with both wrestlers and fans. However, Roberts eventually became more popular with fans. He had rivalries with wrestlers such as the Honky Tonk Man and André the Giant.

Roberts left the WWE in 1992. He temporarily joined the WCW before returning to WWE in 1996. In 2014, he was inducted into the WWE Hall of Fame.

FUN FACT

Jake "The Snake" Roberts had a pet python named Damien.

In 2013, Jake "The Snake" Roberts attended the Chicago Comic and Entertainment Expo in Chicago, Illinois.

THE ROCK

Dwayne "The Rock" Johnson is one of the most famous celebrities to come out of WWE. The son of WWE Hall of Famer Rocky Johnson, The Rock came from a notable wrestling family.

The Rock, *left*, faces off against John Cena at WrestleMania XXVIII in 2012. Cena was one of The Rock's biggest rivals.

In 2015, The Rock was honored for his acting accomplishments at TCL Chinese Theatre in Los Angeles, California. He spoke to fans in front of posters advertising his film *San Andreas*.

He called himself Rocky Maivia, a combination of his dad's name and grandfather's name. This name was shortened to The Rock.

After debuting in 1996, The Rock steadily rose to fame, winning eight WWE Championships. A star of the Attitude Era, The Rock was a heel in the ring. But with his cocky attitude, charisma, and dominance, he gained a large fan base.

In 1999, The Rock became a babyface, portraying one of his most popular characters, The People's Champion. As a good guy, he earned even more fans. The Rock soon became the WWE's top entertainer.

The Rock also found stardom as an actor. He starred in the TV series *Ballers* and in movies such as *Fast & Furious* and *Jumanji*. Eventually, he left wrestling to focus on acting. He occasionally returns to WWE for special events.

FUN FACT

The Rock played college football at the University of Miami.

Seth Rollins celebrates after defeating John Cena in a "Winner Takes All" match at WWE SummerSlam 2015.

SETH ROLLINS

With his signature stomp and a knack for fashion, Seth "Freakin" Rollins earned numerous titles throughout his career. He is the only person to hold the WWE Championship and the United States Championship at the same time.

FUN FACT

When Rollins travels, he carries his wrestling gear and championship belts with him instead of checking them with his luggage.

Rollins made his WWE debut in 2010. He was a member of the Shield stable. After the Shield broke up, Rollins focused on his solo career, portraying both heel and babyface characters. He became a Grand Slam Champion and won an Intercontinental Title at WrestleMania 34 in 2018. The following year, he defeated Brock Lesnar to win the Universal Championship. In 2023, Rollins defeated AJ Styles to win the first new World Heavyweight Championship.

Seth Rollins, *right*, battles Drew McIntyre, *left*, during the second night of WrestleMania 40 in 2024. Rollins ended up losing the match.

JIM ROSS

Jim Ross was the play-by-play announcer on *Monday Night Raw* for almost ten years. He became one of the most famous commentators in pro-wrestling history. He was known for the saying, "Business is about to pick up."

Ross made his debut in 1993. The Oklahoma native was known for wearing a black cowboy hat during matches. He gained experience in both wrestling and commentary after years of calling matches. He has also performed inside the ring from time to time.

FUN FACT

Jim Ross is a fan of the Oklahoma Sooners college football team. He can often be found on the sidelines during their games.

As a commentator, Jim Ross was known for his extensive pro-wrestling knowledge and Southern US accent.

In 2009, Jim Ross, *center*, appeared onstage during an event for the 25th anniversary of the WWE Hall of Fame.

In the mid-2000s, Ross faced off against wrestlers such as Jack Swagger and Triple H. He also competed against fellow announcer Michael Cole. Ross was inducted into the WWE Hall of Fame in 2007. He left the organization in 2013.

Ronda Rousey, *left*, competes against Bethe Correia during the 2015 UFC 190 event in Rio de Janeiro, Brazil. Rousey won the match.

RONDA ROUSEY

When it comes to competitive fighting, Ronda Rousey is hard to beat. In 2008, she won a bronze medal in judo at the Olympic Games. She later became a UFC Hall of Famer and WWE star.

FUN FACT

Ronda Rousey is the first American woman to win an Olympic medal in judo.

Rousey used her background in judo to dominate the UFC. She became the first woman to sign with the mixed martial arts company, and she then won the first UFC Women's

Bantamweight title. In 2018, she became the first woman inducted into the UFC Hall of Fame.

Rousey joined the WWE in 2018. She made an immediate impact, competing in Elimination Chamber 2018 before even signing her Raw contract. It was a memorable debut, as the match was scripted to showcase Rousey's skills.

During WrestleMania 34, Rousey battled Triple H and Stephanie McMahon. She dominated Triple H and ended the match by using a cross-arm move on McMahon. She then teamed up with Kurt Angle to win the Mixed Tag Team Match at WrestleMania 34. In 2023, Rousey was drafted to Raw.

Ronda Rousey smiles after winning the Raw Women's Championship at WWE SummerSlam 2018. She defeated Alexa Bliss to claim the title.

Bruno Sammartino was known for headlining wrestling events at Madison Square Garden in New York City. Some people called Madison Square Garden "The House That Bruno Built."

BRUNO SAMMARTINO

Italian wrestler Bruno Sammartino was the longest-reigning WWE champion. Known as The Italian Superman, he was adored by fans and fellow wrestlers. In 1959, Sammartino set a world record by bench pressing 565 pounds (256 kg). Former WWE CEO Vincent J. McMahon noticed this and persuaded Sammartino to pursue professional wrestling.

In 1963, Sammartino became the second-ever WWE champion when he defeated Buddy Rogers at Madison Square Garden in New York City. He held the title for almost eight years, marking the longest reign of all time. Sammartino lost the title in 1971 but regained it in 1973. He held the title for three and a half years. In his final match, Sammartino teamed up with Hulk Hogan. After retiring from wrestling, Sammartino became a sports broadcaster.

FUN FACT

During World War II, Sammartino hid in the mountains when Nazi forces took over his Italian town.

Bruno Sammartino, *top*, faced off against many well-known wrestlers, such as The Sheik, *right*.

"MACHO MAN" RANDY SAVAGE

"Macho Man" Randy Savage was one of pro wrestling's biggest stars during the 1980s and 1990s. With his flashy costumes, raspy voice, and catchphrase of "Oooh yeah," he was easily recognizable. During his career, the intense wrestler won two WWE championships and four WCW World Championships.

Savage almost pursued baseball over wrestling, signing with the St. Louis Cardinals after high school. However, an injury in the minor leagues cut Savage's baseball career short. Instead, Savage made his pro-wrestling debut in 1973. He joined the WWE in 1985. Savage hired a female manager, Miss Elizabeth, who became his real-life wife and was called the First Lady of Wrestling. Savage won his first WWE title in 1986, defeating Tito Santana.

"Macho Man" Randy Savage's real name was Randy Poffo. He began wrestling under the name "The Spider."

Savage formed a wrestling duo with

"Macho Man" Randy Savage was famous for his bold, colorful wrestling costumes. He often wore large sunglasses, sparkly capes, and outfits with fringe.

FUN FACT

Savage married his manager, the First Lady of Wrestling, in front of fans at SummerSlam 1991.

Hulk Hogan. But the wrestlers turned on each other, and Hogan defeated Savage at WrestleMania V to win the 1989 WWE Championship. Savage died in 2011. He was inducted into the WWE Hall of Fame in 2015.

RICKY STEAMBOAT

Ricky Steamboat was a favorite among both fans and other wrestlers. He made his AWA debut in 1976 under the name Richard Blood. He initially specialized in tag team competitions, partnering with Jay Youngblood in the mid-Atlantic area.

In 1985, he entered WWF as a babyface, changing his name to Ricky Steamboat. People nicknamed him the Dragon, and he was known for wearing Japanese-inspired costumes. Steamboat was the WWE's Intercontinental Champion in 1987 and won the NWA World Championship in 1989.

Steamboat's most notable fights were against Ric Flair. In 1989, he competed in a three-match series with Flair. They had

Ricky Steamboat, *pictured*, was known for having memorable battles against wrestlers such as Jake "The Snake" Roberts, Ric Flair, and "Macho Man" Randy Savage.

FUN FACT

Steamboat's son, Richie Steamboat, was also a pro wrestler.

Ricky Steamboat, *right*, faces off against Don "The Magnificent" Muraco, *left*, during a 1985 match. The two wrestlers had a feud.

three epic battles lasting between 23 and 55 minutes. Fans loved watching Flair, a heel, face off against the heroic Steamboat. Steamboat retired from professional wrestling in 1994.

Sting competed at WrestleMania 31 in 2015. It was his first time competing in the event.

STING

Sting became one of WCW's most recognizable stars during the 1990s. Called "The Franchise of WCW," he was known for his distinctive blonde hair, face paint, and neon costumes. His charisma and skill in the ring made him popular with fans. His moves and costumes often featured scorpion images.

Sting's popularity soared in 1996 when he began battling against nWo. He changed his look, wearing black and white face paint and clothes to show his darker side.

FUN FACT

Sting has the most pay-per-view appearances of any WCW wrestler with 99.

Sting didn't fight for more than a year, building up mystery and excitement for when he finally competed against nWo. He returned in 1997 to fight and defeat nWo leader "Hollywood" Hulk Hogan. Sting continued to feud with nWo when he joined the nWo Wolfpac stable.

Sting appeared in his first WWE event in 2014. He won six WCW World Titles, three WCW Tag Team Championships, two WCW International World Titles, and two United States Championships. He was inducted into the WWE Hall of Fame in 2016.

Sting, *left*, faces off against Swerve Strickland during the 2023 AEW All In event in London, England.

TRISH STRATUS

Trish Stratus redefined what it meant to be a female wrestler. She proved that women in the pro-wrestling world were more than just attractive faces—they were skilled athletes and competitors. She was a tough manager and wrestler, often playing a heel.

Stratus joined WWE as a manager in 2000. The next year, she began competing. One of the Canadian wrestler's first matches came at No Way Out 2001, when she competed against Stephanie McMahon. Both women were managers and lacked wrestling experience, but they delivered an intense fight. Stratus lost, but she won fans with her charisma and performance skills.

Trish Stratus's real name is Patricia Anne Stratigeas. She debuted in WWE as the manager of the tag team Test and Albert.

Stratus launched her career at the 2001 Survivor Series, defeating five competitors to win the women's title. The victory made her the face of women's wrestling. During her time in WWE,

Trish Stratus, *center*, battles Melina and Mickey James during the WWE Raw Superslam event in 2006.

Stratus became one of the organization's most accomplished female wrestlers, winning seven Women's Championships.

Stratus retired from wrestling in 2006. Her last match was at Unforgiven, where she defeated Lita to win the Women's Championship. Since retiring, Stratus has made several appearances on WWE. She was inducted into the WWE Hall of Fame in 2013.

FUN FACT

Before becoming a wrestler, Trish Stratus worked as a fitness model.

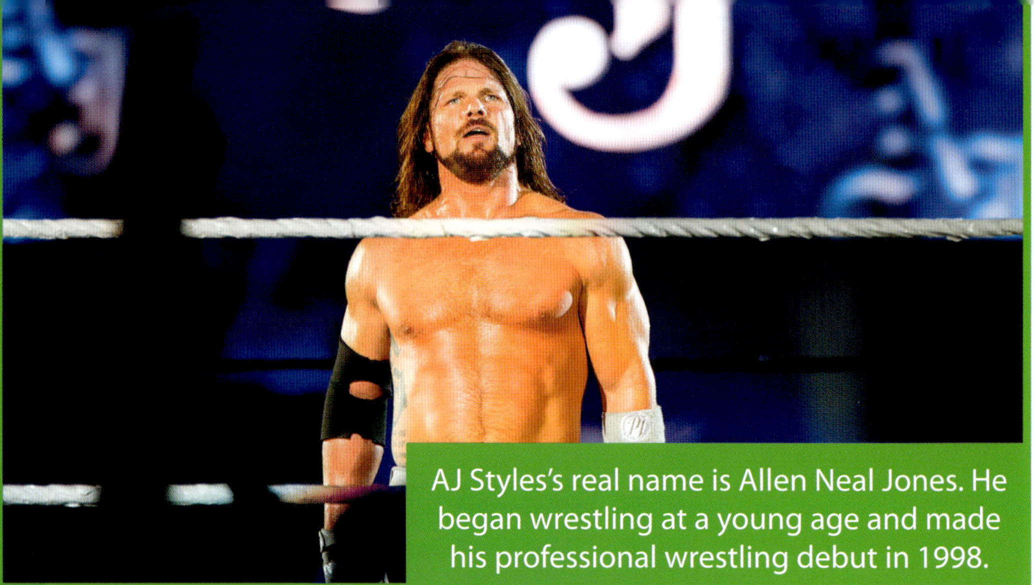

AJ Styles's real name is Allen Neal Jones. He began wrestling at a young age and made his professional wrestling debut in 1998.

AJ STYLES

Nicknamed "the Phenomenal One," AJ Styles used creative aerial moves, confidence, and skill to defeat opponents and gain fans. He made his WWE debut in 2016 at the Royal Rumble. Styles won the WWE Championship twice and has called SmackDown "The House that AJ Styles Built."

FUN FACT

Styles named one of his children after Christopher Daniels, his friend and fellow wrestler.

Styles is a crowd favorite as a babyface, especially when he takes on top wrestlers such as Chris Jericho, Roman Reigns, and Daniel Bryan. However, he does some of his best performances as a heel. The WWE star has become known for feuds with John Cena, Dean Ambrose, and Shane McMahon.

One of the wrestler's biggest accomplishments was winning a Grand Slam Championship in 2021. Styles is known for using signature moves such as the Styles Clash, the Calf Crusher, and the Phenomenal Forearm. In 2024, he was still competing.

AJ Styles flips over opponent Cody Rhodes at the Backlash France event in 2024.

TRIPLE H

Triple H is considered WWE royalty both inside and outside of the ring. As a 14-time World Champion and cofounder of the D-Generation X stable, he had a Hall of Fame career. Outside of his wrestling storylines, he shapes the future of the WWE as the organization's chief content officer. He is also married to Stephanie McMahon.

FUN FACT

In 2021, Triple H underwent a heart surgery after suffering heart failure.

Triple H appeared onstage during the first night of WrestleMania 40 in 2024.

When Triple H joined WWE in 1995, he was known as Hunter Hearst Helmsley, which was later shortened to Triple H. This character was an elitist whose finishing move was the Pedigree. Triple H's popularity rose when he joined The Kliq and founded D-Generation X in 1997. This earned him main event appearances. By 1999, he was considered one of the top WWE wrestlers.

In addition to his World Championships, Triple H has won two Royal Rumble Matches. Triple H retired from wrestling in 2022 at WrestleMania 38. At the event, he left his boots in the ring. This is a common way for wrestlers to end their careers.

Triple H celebrates after winning the WWE Championship title at WrestleMania 25 in 2009. He defeated Randy Orton to retain the title.

The Ultimate Warrior was known for his colorful wrestling costumes. He often wore face paint and neon colors.

ULTIMATE WARRIOR

> **FUN FACT**
>
> The Ultimate Warrior legally changed his name to "Warrior."

The Ultimate Warrior made his WWE debut in 1987 and quickly stood out. He ran full speed toward the ring before matches, forcing the audience to take notice of him. The aggressive wrestler spoke in riddles and was known for being intense during matches. The Ultimate Warrior also wore a face-paint mask in the ring.

One of the Ultimate Warrior's biggest victories came in 1990 at WrestleMania VI, when he defeated Hulk Hogan to win the WWE Championship. The victory allowed the Ultimate Warrior to hold the Intercontinental and WWE titles at the same time. The Ultimate Warrior was inducted into the WWE Hall of Fame on April 6, 2014. He passed away three days later.

The Ultimate Warrior, *left*, was often involved in battles and storylines with Hulk Hogan, *right*. The two wrestlers had a rivalry.

UNDERTAKER

Undertaker was a dominant force in the WWE, acting as one of its longest-lasting characters. He made his debut at Survivor Series in 1990. His WWE career went on to span three decades.

Undertaker's main gimmick was The Deadman, a menacing character. This undead, scary persona struck fear in opponents. As part of his storyline, Undertaker often teamed up with his half brother Kane, competing as the Brothers of Destruction. Undertaker used other gimmicks, but The Deadman was his most popular.

Undertaker, *right*, performs his "Snake Eyes" move on opponent Shawn Michaels during WrestleMania XXVI in 2010.

Undertaker, *top*, battles Brock Lesnar during WrestleMania 30. Many fans were shocked when Lesnar defeated Undertaker in the match.

Undertaker earned numerous titles, including WWE and World Heavyweight Championships. However, he was best known for his long undefeated streak at WrestleMania. After winning his first 21 matches at the event, his streak ended at WrestleMania 30 in 2014 when he lost to Brock Lesnar. Undertaker retired at Survivor Series in November 2020. He was inducted into the WWE Hall of Fame in 2022.

FUN FACT

Undertaker played college basketball at Texas Wesleyan University before becoming a pro wrestler.

Fritz Von Erich, *pictured*, trained his sons to become wrestlers at a young age.

THE VON ERICHS

The Von Erichs were a prominent pro-wrestling family in the 1980s and 1990s. The Texan family included Fritz Von Erich and his sons Kevin, David, Kerry, Mike, and Chris, who all used the ring name Von Erich. Fritz Von Erich's career flourished in the 1960s and 1970s, and he became known for using a wrestling hold called the Iron Claw. Later, he served as president of WCCW.

In WCCW, Kevin, David, and Kerry Von Erich often competed together and had a feud against The Fabulous Freebirds. Each brother developed his own persona and gimmicks. Kevin was known for wrestling barefoot in the ring, while David wore cowboy hats. Kerry was the most well-known of the Von Erich brothers. He famously defeated Ric Flair to claim the 1984 NWA World Heavyweight Championship title. In 1990, Kerry began competing in WWF under the name the Texas Tornado.

As of 2024, Kevin is the only living member of the Von Erich family wrestlers. In 2009, the Von Erichs were inducted into the WWE Hall of Fame. Kevin represented his family at the induction ceremony.

FUN FACT

In 2023, the production company A24 released a highly-praised film about the Von Erichs called *The Iron Claw*.

Kevin Von Erich, *third from right*, does the Iron Claw move with actors from *The Iron Claw* at the film's premiere in 2023. The move involves putting a hand over an opponent's forehead and squeezing it.

MAE YOUNG

Mae Young's wrestling career began in 1939. She started competing during World War II, when more areas in the United States started offering the sport. She was a pioneer for women's pro wrestling, helping to popularize it. Young was the first US Women's Champion too.

Young's biggest rival was Mildred Burke. The two wrestlers traveled to Japan in 1954, becoming two of the first female wrestlers to compete in post-war Japan. Young was also a notable wrestling trainer. She trained star wrestlers such as the Fabulous Moolah. The longest-reigning champion in pro-wrestling history, Moolah became the first woman inducted into the WWE Hall of Fame.

Mae Young, *right*, battles opponent Mae Weston, *center*, during a 1943 match. Young was often called "The Queen" or "The Great Mae Young."

Mae Young, *right*, and her trainee The Fabulous Moolah, *left*, attended the premiere of a wrestling documentary film in 2004.

Young competed in events in the 1990s and 2000s, when she was in her 70s. She was inducted into the WWE Hall of Fame in 2008. She was only the third woman to become a Hall of Famer. Young died in January 2014. WWE fans held a standing ovation to honor her.

FUN FACT

In high school, Young earned a spot on the wrestling team. She was the only girl on the team.

GLOSSARY

amateur
A person who does something for enjoyment without getting paid.

charisma
Charm or appeal.

commissioner
In pro wrestling, an official who arranges matches, sets rules, and oversees events.

controversy
A disagreement or debate about which people have strong views.

draft
In sports, to choose eligible players to join a professional team, league, or organization.

headline
To be featured as the main star of an event or sports match.

hold
A wrestling move that involves grabbing one's opponent and trying to hold them down.

intimidate
To frighten or threaten someone.

notorious
Well-known for negative or controversial reasons.

persona
A role, character, or personality that someone presents to others; wrestlers use personas while competing.

promoter
A person who promotes, organizes, schedules, and advertises wrestling events.

retain
In sports, to win a trophy, event, or title again after having been the last person to win it.

roster
An official list of players on a sports team.

signature
Describing something that is associated with a person's unique style or identity.

submission
In pro wrestling, when a wrestler ends a match, taps the mat, or tells the referee they are quitting.

troupes
Groups of traveling entertainers or performers.

valet
A name for a female wrestling manager who accompanies a male wrestler.

TO LEARN MORE

FURTHER READINGS

Black, Jake. *WWE Superstar Handbook: The Essential Facts and Stats on More than 300 WWE Superstars!* DK, 2021.

Monnig, Alex. *Andre the Giant*. Abdo, 2024.

Monnig, Alex. *Ronda Rousey*. Abdo, 2024.

ONLINE RESOURCES

Booklinks
NONFICTION NETWORK
FREE! ONLINE NONFICTION RESOURCES

To learn more about professional wrestling, please visit **abdobooklinks.com** or scan this QR code. These links are routinely monitored and updated to provide the most current information available.

INDEX

PHOTO CREDITS

Cover Photos: Etsuo Hara/Getty Images Sport/Getty Images, front (Asuka); Ronald Martinez/Getty Images Sport/Getty Images, front (Charlotte Flair); Suzanne Cordeiro/Corbis Sport/Getty Images, front (John Cena); Gerardo Zavala/Jam Media/LatinContent Editorial/Getty Images, front (Rey Mysterio); Hulton Archive/Getty Images, front (Steve Austin); WWE/Getty Images Sport/Getty Images, front (The Rock), back (Bianca Belair, Seth Rollins); Kevin Mazur/WireImage/Getty Images, front (The Undertaker)

Interior Photos: Tim Nwachukwu/Getty Images Sport/Getty Images, 1; Ronald Martinez/Getty Images Sport/Getty Images, 2–3, 74, 75; Old Books Images/Alamy, 4; Hirarchivum Press/Alamy, 5; ullstein bild/Getty Images, 6; Bettmann/Getty Images, 7, 8, 102, 167; Marty Lederhandler/AP Images, 9; John Smock/Sipa Press/Newscom, 10; Adam Scull/PHOTOlink/MediaPunch Inc/Alamy, 11; Erik S. Lesser/AP Images, 12; Kevin Mazur/WireImage/Getty Images, 13, 86; Tom "Mo" Moschella/Icon Sportswire, 14; John Barrett/Globe Photos/ZUMA Press, Inc./Alamy, 15; Paul Abell/WWE/AP Images, 16, 28, 66, 144; Shutterstock Images, 17, 22, 41, 47, 67, 79, 105, 116, 129, 131, 137, 138–139, 148, 159, 164, 173, 176; Sankei Archive/Getty Images, 18; Joern Pollex/Bongarts/Getty Images, 19; Cora Veltman/Sportico/Getty Images, 20; WWE/Getty Images Sport/Getty Images, 21, 23, 24, 43, 48, 49, 60, 117, 118, 149, 150, 151, 153, 161, 177, 178; Frank Jansky/Icon Sportswire/AP Images, 25; JP Yim/Getty Images Entertainment/Getty Images, 26, 160; Bruce Bennett Studios/Getty Images Studios/Getty Images, 27, 97, 156; Don Feria/WWE/AP Images, 28–29, 57, 172–173; Yukio Hiraku/AFLO/Newscom, 30, 136, 154; Richard Drew/AP Images, 31; Michael Lipchitz/AP Images, 32–33; Olivier Andrivon/Icon Sport/Getty Images, 33; Alex Bierens de Haan/Getty Images Sport/Getty Images, 34, 152; Etsuo Hara/Getty Images Sport/Getty Images, 35, 39, 55, 103, 125; Leon Halip/WireImage/Getty Images, 36; S_Bukley/Newscom, 37; Sylvain Lefevre/Getty Images Sport/Getty Images, 38, 42, 54; Gaye Gerard/Getty Images Entertainment/Getty Images, 40; Charles Krupa/AP Images, 44; Jason Koerner/Getty Images Entertainment/Getty Images, 45; Jim R. Bounds/WWE/AP Images, 46; KMazur/WireImage/Getty Images, 50; Gabe Ginsberg/Getty Images Entertainment/Getty Images, 51; Jonathan Bachman/WWE/AP Images, 52, 53, 138, 183; Moses Robinson/Getty Images Entertainment/Getty Images, 56, 108; Nancy Kaszerman/ZUMA Press, Inc./Alamy Live News/Alamy, 58; Vinnie Zuffante/Archive Photos/Getty Images, 59; John Barrett/PHOTOlink/CelebrityArchaeology.com/Alamy, 61, 64, 92, 94–95, 95, 96; Fayez Nureidine/AFP/Getty Images, 62; George Napolitano/FilmMagic/Getty Images, 63, 134, 155; Rick Scuteri/WWE/AP Images, 65; Djamilla Rosa Cochran/WireImage/Getty Images, 68; Mark Mainz/Getty Images Entertainment/Getty Images, 69; George Napolitano/SplashNews/Newscom, 70; Brandon Wade/WWE/AP Images, 71; Paul Natkin/Archive Photos/Getty Images, 72; The Stanley Weston Archive/Archive Photos/Getty Images, 73, 184; Jeff Siner/The Charlotte Observer/AP Images, 76; Snapper Media/Splash News/Newscom, 77; WENN Rights Ltd/Alamy, 78; George Napolitano/MediaPunch Inc/Alamy, 80; Bobby Bank/Getty Images Entertainment/Getty Images, 81; Archive PL/Alamy, 82; Phillip Harrington/Alamy, 83; MPIRock/MediaPunch/Archive Photos/Getty Images, 84; Jerod Harris/Getty Images Entertainment/Getty Images, 85; Peter Kramer/Getty Images Entertainment/Getty Images, 87; Matt Roberts/ZUMA Press/Icon Sportswire, 88, 89; Rick Scuteri/AP Images, 90, 182; Robert Clark/AP Images, 91; Bruce Bennett/Getty Images, 93, 168, 169, 170, 170–171; John Barrett/PHOTOlink/MediaPunch/IPX/AP Images, 98; John Barrett/PHOTOlink/Newscom, 99, 109, 114, 146, 180, 181; George Pimentel/WireImage/Getty Images, 100, 119, 133, 141; Chris Carlson/AP Images, 100–101; Hulton Archive/Getty Images, 104; Chris Ryan/Corbis Sport/Getty Images, 106; Don Arnold/WireImage/Getty Images, 107, 175; Matt Roberts/ZUMA Wire/ZUMA Press, Inc./Alamy Live News/Alamy, 110; John Palmer/MediaPunch/IPX/AP Images, 111; Steve W. Grayson/Newsmakers/Hulton Archive/Getty Images, 112–113; ParisaMichelle/SplashNews/Newscom, 113; John Barrett/PHOTOlink/MediaPunch Inc/Alamy, 115; Ethan Miller/Getty Images Entertainment/Getty Images, 120–121; Tom Strattman/AP Images, 121; Carrie Devorah/CD1/WENN/Newscom, 122; Victoria Arocho/AP Images, 123; Marc Pfitzenreuter/Getty Images Sport/Getty Images, 124; Guillermo Grandos/GGV/SPO/NOTIMEX/Newscom, 126; Elsa/Getty Images Sport/Getty Images, 127; kolvenbach/Alamy, 128; Marc Serota/WWE/AP Images, 130; Steve Granitz/WireImage/Getty Images, 132; Gustavo Caballero/Getty Images Entertainment/Getty Images, 135; Elsa Hasch/Allsport/Getty Images Sport/Getty Images, 140; John Shearer/WireImage for BWR Public Relations/WireImage/Getty Images, 142; Bill Olive/Getty Images Entertainment/Getty Images, 143; Marc Serota/Wrestlemania/AP Images, 145; Cory McDonald/Florida Memory, 147; Daniel Boczarski/Getty Images Entertainment/Getty Images, 157; Ron Elkman/Sports Imagery/Getty Images Sport/Getty Images, 158; J. Shearer/WireImage/Getty Images, 162; Bob Levey/WireImage/Getty Images, 163, 179; George Napolitano/MediaPunch/IPX/AP Images, 165; Focus On Sport/Getty Images, 166; Phillip Massey/FilmMagic/Getty Images, 174; Amanda Edwards/WireImage/Getty Images, 185; GF/AP Images, 186; Jim Spellman/WireImage/Getty Images, 187

ABDOBOOKS.COM

Published by Abdo Reference, a division of ABDO, PO Box 398166, Minneapolis, Minnesota 55439.

Printed in China.
102024
012025

THIS BOOK CONTAINS RECYCLED MATERIALS

Editor: Laura Stickney
Series Designer: Colleen McLaren
Production Designer: Laura Kuchar

LIBRARY OF CONGRESS CONTROL NUMBER: 2024938494

PUBLISHER'S CATALOGING-IN-PUBLICATION DATA

Names: Gerard, Mary, author.
Title: The professional wrestling encyclopedia / by Mary Gerard
Description: Minneapolis, Minnesota: Abdo Reference, 2025 | Series: Sports encyclopedias | Includes online resources and index.
Identifiers: ISBN 9781098296117 (lib. bdg.) | ISBN 9798384917113 (eBook)
Subjects: LCSH: World Wide Wrestling Federation--Juvenile literature. | Professional sports--Juvenile literature. | Athletics--Juvenile literature. | Wrestling--Juvenile literature. | Sports--History--Juvenile literature.
Classification: DDC 796.812--dc23